Crosscurrents / MODERN CRITIQUES

Harry T. Moore, *General Editor*

Accelerated Grimace

Expressionism in the
American Drama of the 1920s

Mardi Valgemae

WITH A PREFACE BY
Harry T. Moore

SOUTHERN ILLINOIS UNIVERSITY PRESS
Carbondale and Edwardsville

FEFFER & SIMONS, INC.
London and Amsterdam

For Marë

Contents

Mardi Valgemae's Accelerated Grimace: Expressionism in the American Drama of the 1920s *is the first full ex-ploration of this subject. But it has the impact of more than a merely pioneering book, for it deals with its material in a rounded way, giving a full picture and at the same time presenting important judgments.*

We have had various studies of the influence of the French theater upon the American, and it is amazing that, before Mr. Valgemae, no one has thought of a lengthy investigation of the effects of German expres-sionism, as it flourished in the 1920s, upon American writers of that time.

As I have indicated elsewhere (Twentieth-Century German Literature, first published 1967),

> Expressionism, with its explosive syntax, its disinte-grating forms, and its panoramic simultanieties, had a kinship with many other modern-art movements, in-cluding futurism and cubism; it borrowed from Rim-baud and the French symbolists, it was influenced by Dostoevsky and Strindberg, and it was motivated by Freud's explorations of the unconscious. . . . The expressionists felt that they created rather than merely reproduced, and that they were reacting against what they regarded as the predominantly sur-

face approaches of such nineteenth-century movements as naturalism and impressionism. For the most
part these were concerned, for all their differences,
with material aspects; the expressionists regarded
themselves as concentrating upon the spiritual. Therefore they could throw out the customary realistic devices of representation and could violate grammar as
well as the theatrical conventions of verisimilitudes:
in the expressionist drama the thoughts of a character
could be presented by soliloquy or by slides thrown
upon a screen.

Mr. Valgemae in his introductory chapter mentions
the influence of Strindberg upon the expressionists, and
refers to George Büchner's Woyzeck (1836–37) as well
as various other ancestral authors and their works. But
like most historians he finds expressionism in fullest
bloom in the Germany of the 1920s, particularly in the
plays of Georg Kaiser. Yet early in that decade, as Mr.
Valgemae demonstrates, American writers were turning
out expressionistic dramas. He deals at length with
Eugene O'Neill in that phase of his work, and also gives
a good amount of space to such playwrights as Elmer
Rice and John Howard Lawson.

Surprisingly, a tremendous number of authors wrote
expressionistic plays at this time, including such popular
surface-dramatists as Channing Pollack. The naturalistic
novelist Theodore Dreiser contributed his quota, and so
did Upton Sinclair and John Dos Passos. The humorist
Ring Lardner even joined in the fun.

By the late 1930s, depression time, the movement had
come to a stop, though occasionally some of its techniques were used, notably in such productions as the
WPA Theater's The Living Newspaper, called a docu-
mentary, though it used some of the devices of expressionism.

Mr. Valgemae gives a valuable account of the movement's influence upon the theater today. Altogether, his book is a rich one, of a kind we very much need. Mr. Valgemae, who is an Associate Professor of English at the Herbert H. Lehman College, City University of New York, has a fine sense of the historical: he not only finds the facts but also knows how to link them together to create a fascinating story, accurate, lively, and permanently valuable. This volume will be most useful to students of the theater and of course to all who are interested in the literature of our time.

HARRY T. MOORE

Southern Illinois University
November 10, 1971

Introduction

Dawn was breaking over the housetops on Washington Square as two young men stopped for a moment by the fountain to bid each other good-bye. Both were in the frame of mind which is called happy for a long time after the real enjoyment that belongs to mild potations and unstinted argument and song is evaporated. Though neither had taken enough to intoxicate, they held each other closely embraced, keeping up by a tacit effort the convivial spirit which, so far, had inspired the meetings of the Expressionists.

This might well be a description of New York's Greenwich Village in the decade following the explosive Armory Show of modern art in 1913, as two bohemians are leaving an "Evening" at Mabel Dodge's famed salon. Or it might be a romantic account of the Provincetown Players in the 1920s, or even of the Theatre Guild, which in its early years produced Continental experimentalists, or of the New Playwrights' Theatre, active when the expressionist movement in the American drama had reached its height. Actually, it is the opening paragraph of Charles DeKay's novel *The Bohemian*, which was published in 1878, decades before the birth of expressionism as a historically recorded aesthetic force.

In less than fifty years, DeKay's fictional account of a small group of writers, artists, and bohemians who called themselves the Expressionists and haunted the environs of New York's Washington Square became a reality—at least in geography and terminology. The word *expressionism* entered the vocabulary of American theatregoers in the spring of 1922 with the New York productions of Eugene O'Neill's *The Hairy Ape* and Georg Kaiser's *From Morn to Midnight*. And although no Village group in the twenties was formally known by that name, the term was frequently used in reference to several off-Broadway theatrical organizations of the period. The Provincetown theatre, for example, was called by the *New York Times* "Macdougal Street's foremost expressionistic playhouse," and when two members of the New Playwrights' Theatre quarreled in print over aesthetic matters, a headline in the *Herald Tribune* proclaimed a "Civil War Between the Expressionists."

Though expressionism was the new movement in the American drama of the 1920s, it has not yet been comprehensively studied. No book exists on the subject. Consequently there is considerable confusion as to what constitutes an expressionist play. The fact that early commentators on American expressionism sometimes called it "impressionism" has not helped to clarify matters. This confusion has been compounded by the tendency on the part of certain critics to apply the term *expressionism* to almost any modern departure from realism.

Yet, as this study endeavors to show, expressionism denotes a specific formal technique that evolved in a clearly demonstrable historical pattern. Hence the emphasis in this work on formal and historical considerations. At the same time it must be kept in mind that our interest in expressionism is not solely for the sake of praising or condemning a play according to how it fits into that movement. On the contrary, we should be concerned with technique only insofar as it illuminates specific dramatic works. Furthermore, our interest in expressionism ought to go deeper than antiquarian curiosity. For much of what is happening in the American theatre of today—in the lofts and churches and coffee houses of off-off-Broadway—is firmly rooted in the expressionist tradition.

Since expressionism in the drama is closely linked to the visual aspects of stage presentation, several unpublished plays have been considered at the expense of published works that have not altered the image of American drama. Thus all dates, unless otherwise noted, are production dates and, in the case of native plays, refer specifically to New York productions.

I am grateful to the Research Committee of the University of California, Los Angeles, for a travel grant, and to the Regents of the University of California for a Summer Faculty Fellowship that enabled me to devote my time exclusively to writing.

I should like to thank the staffs of the following libraries for their generous assistance: the Dartmouth College Library, the Egri-Cornell Writers Workshop, the Lilly Library of Indiana University, the Library of Congress, the Berg and the Theatre Collections of the New York Public Library, the Princeton University Library, the UCLA Research Library, the Walter Hampden Memorial Library, and the American Literature Collection of the Yale University Library, whose Curator, Mr. Donald Gallup, has helped me to secure permissions.

For their suggestions and critical insights I am indebted to Professors William W. Melnitz, Blake R. Nevius, Andrezej T. Wirth, and especially Leon Howard, to whose guidance and encouragement I owe more than these lines can express. For sharing with me their time and much valuable information, I wish to thank the late John Dos Passos, Michael B. Folsom, Paul Green, John Howard Lawson, the late Kenneth Macgowan, Albert Maltz, the late Elmer Rice, George Sklar, and Mary Heaton Vorse.

Permission to quote from the unpublished letters of Eugene O'Neill has been granted by Mrs. Carlotta O'Neill. Permission to quote from the O'Neill-Block letter is by the courtesy of the Walter Hampden Memorial Library at The Players, New York.

Three chapters in this volume appeared in part or in

different form in the following publications and are here reprinted with permission of the publishers: Chapter 3 originally appeared in slightly different form under the title "O'Neill and German Expressionism" in *Modern Drama*, 10 (1967), 111–23; a portion of Chapter 5 appeared as an article on Elmer Rice's *The Subway*, copyright by *The Explicator*, No. 62 (1967); half of Chapter 7 was published under the title "Civil War Among the Expressionists: John Howard Lawson and the *Pinwheel* Controversy" in the *Educational Theatre Journal*, 20 (March 1968), 8–14.

MARDI VALGEMAE

Herbert H. Lehman College
The City University of New York
August 20, 1971

1

The Spell of Expressionism

In the fall of 1926 a new theatrical organization was founded in New York. Called the Theatre Creative, it announced as its purpose the encouragement of worthy artists and declared its opposition to "the creative inspiration and intellectual stimulus from the dramatists of Europe." The group had executive offices on Fifth Avenue, Mayor James J. Walker acted as the chairman of its advisory board, and among the board members were Governor Arthur H. Moore of New Jersey and Professor William Lyon Phelps of Yale. On the day following this announcement, the *New York Times* printed an editorial on the native Theatre Creative. It was the opinion of the *Times* that opposition to European ideas was foolish, even though New York theatre audiences "have found it hard to swallow local versions of European expressionism." The editorial went on to comment on one of the controversial playwrights of the day: "So considerable a figure as EUGENE O'NEILL, as he has wandered in the footsteps of the Berlin experimentalists, has given occasion for serious headshaking." [1]

Who were the Berlin experimentalists? And how serious was the charge that recent formal innovations in European dramaturgy were corrupting the work of native playwrights? Answers to these questions require an investigation of the avant-garde movement in the American drama of the 1920s as well as an exploration of its

1

foreign roots. For expressionism, like most new developments in early twentieth-century art, music, and literature, originated in Europe.

The echoes of Ibsen's Nora's slamming the door of her husband's doll's house in 1879 had scarcely faded when symbolist playwrights and such pioneers of imaginative stagecraft as Adolphe Appia and Edward Gordon Craig began to undermine the foundations of the realistic stage. In their efforts to retheatricalize the theatre, both Appia and Craig urged the simplification and purification of scene design and stressed the importance of a unified theatrical effect that would bring out the inner life of the play. The essential life of the soul that exists beyond everyday reality also formed an important part of the dramatic theory of the Belgian playwright Maurice Maeterlinck. In Russia the stagecraft of such experimental directors as Vsevolod Meyerhold, Alexander Tairov, and Eugene Vakhtangov supplemented the work of radical playwrights. Nikolai Evreinov dramatized his concept of "monodrama" in a number of plays, including *The Theatre of the Soul* (1912), and Leonid Andreyev gave concrete form to the inner world of man in such works as *The Black Maskers* (1908). From Italy came futurism and the theatre of the grotesque, which culminated in the work of Luigi Pirandello.

Yet the most turbulent of these new artistic currents that cleansed the backwaters of realistic stagecraft and dramaturgy was German expressionism. Employing the magic of the forms, movements, sounds, and colors of a stylized theatre, expressionism attempted to penetrate through life's surface reality and portray man's inner world. In order to present subjective states on the stage, a radical change in dramatic form became necessary. Techniques by which objectification is intensified through distortion resulted, and the consequent dreamlike quality became one of the identifying characteristics of expressionist drama. Nightmarish visual images controlled the action; compressed syntax led to an abbreviated pattern of speech; three-dimensional, psychologically developed characters yielded to exaggerated caricatures or abstract types; coherent structure gave way to episodic and often disconnected *Stationen*, or brief scenes.

Like romanticism, expressionism does not lend itself to precise definition. In attempting to gauge the impact of this European movement on American drama, the picture becomes even more blurred, because only a few Continental expressionist plays found their way into our theatres. The American temperament was at that time not receptive to many of the philosophical and hence thematic excesses of Continental expressionism. Thus American dramatists were interested primarily in utilizing the techniques of expressionist dramaturgy. To complicate matters further, in the case of several native playwrights, notably Eugene O'Neill, Elmer Rice, and John Howard Lawson, acquaintance with the new mode either preceded American productions of these plays or was based on contacts with the German expressionist film. It should also be noted that the foreign plays recognized by the more advanced American critics as belonging to the expressionist movement were almost exclusively German. Plays by Strindberg and Andreyev, for example, were generally excluded from this classification. The brief account of Continental expressionism that follows is, therefore, consciously limited to a formal consideration of those works that penetrated into the American theatre and enhanced the development of expressionism in American drama.

Notwithstanding Charles DeKay's fictional use of the term in nineteenth-century America, the word *expressionism* was apparently first applied to a modern work of art in France, where Julien-Auguste Hervé used it in 1901 to designate a cycle of his paintings.[2] Soon the term was employed to distinguish Henri Matisse and other post-impressionist painters from the impressionists. In Germany *Die Brücke* and *Der Blaue Reiter* "expressionists," as these painters were sometimes called, drew inspiration from the works of Vincent van Gogh, Paul Gauguin, and Edvard Munch, and (along with their independent colleagues) carried on the rebellion against the representation of visual reality as perceived by the senses. For instead of the artist's impressions of nature, they were concerned with his expression of himself. As Wassily Kandinsky, author of several experimental plays and one of the leaders of the *Blaue Reiter* group, observed in his theoretical work, *Concerning the Spiritual in Art* (1912), "that is beautiful which is produced by internal necessity, which springs from the soul." [3]

From the visual arts, the term *expressionism* found its way into literary criticism and was given further currency with the production of Walter Hasenclever's play *The Son* (*Der Sohn*) in 1916. In 1917 writer Kasimir Edschmid delivered a lecture, "Concerning Poetic Expressionism," in which he pointed out that the new artist loathes the mere recording of the impressions that an object makes on him. Instead, he endeavors to express the inner meaning: "Facts have meaning only so long as the hand of the artist penetrates them in order to grasp that which lies behind them." Edschmid went on to state that to the artist a house, for example, is no longer merely an object consisting of stone, ugly or beautiful; it has to be looked at until its true form is recognized, until it becomes liberated from the restraints of false reality, until everything that is latent within is expressed. "The world is here," declared Edschmid; "it would be meaningless to reproduce it. To seek it out in its last convulsions, its intrinsic essence and to create it anew—that is the greatest mission of art." The following year Edschmid lectured on the importance of the soul: "In our day the road of poetry leads from the body to the soul, from the social classes to the people, from the outer shell to the spirit." Similarly, the theorists of the avant-garde *Sturm* circle of artists defined expressionism as "the spiritual movement of a time that places inner experience above external life." [4]

The concern with inner experience—art as subjective emotion rather than objective mimesis—links expressionism to romanticism, and certain characteristics of dramatic expressionism can be traced to Greek tragedy, the medieval moralities, and the plays of Shakespeare. Yet for the direct sources of the new drama we must turn to the work of three nineteenth-century dramatists whose plays were staged with enthusiasm at the time of the emergence of German expressionism.

Georg Büchner, a German scientist and political revolutionary, who died at the age of twenty-three, wrote *Woyzeck* in 1836–37. This tragedy of a common soldier who murders his mistress in a fit of jealousy did not receive a production until 1913. It is now regarded as one of the seminal plays of the nineteenth century. Instead of merely presenting the surface story, Büchner attempts to record the tension and struggle within Woyzeck's mind. With the action taking place in more than twenty short and swiftly moving scenes, the work is nervously tense and exclamatory; at times the dialogue becomes highly compressed, and most of the characters, who are known simply by their rank or profession, are exaggerated to the point of caricature. Animals assume human characteristics, and Büchner anticipates the grotesque tone of expressionism (though he does not create it visually) in scenes such as the one in which the protagonist, about to stab his mistress, refers to the red moon as a sword washed in blood.

If Büchner is one of the earliest direct ancestors of German expressionism, then Frank (christened Benjamin Franklin) Wedekind is its stepfather. Influenced by Büchner, whom he greatly admired, Wedekind wrote *Spring's Awakening* (*Frühlings Erwachen*) in 1890–91. It was not performed until 1906, and then only in a bowdlerized version. A frank portrayal of the sexual awakening of adolescents, the play (which was closed after a single performance in New York in 1917) anticipates expressionistic distortion in the scene in which a dead man with his head under his arm and a Masked Gentleman represent a character's inner struggle between suicidal thoughts and the life instinct. Other protoexpressionist elements in the play include two-dimensional characters, heightened speech, and the rapid change of numerous short scenes. Early expressionism manifests itself also in Wedekind's "Lulu" tragedies, in which the heroine represents the abstraction of the female of the species who lives by sexual instincts. In the prologue of *The Earth Spirit* (*Erdgeist*, 1898; staged in New York in 1925 as *The Loves of Lulu*) the playwright introduces the characters as if they were animals in a menagerie, among which Lulu appears as a beautiful but deadly serpent. As Walter H. Sokel has remarked, "Here, as in all other Expressionist works, distortion reveals essence." [5]

Though Büchner's as well as Wedekind's influence on the later drama is considerable, the real father of German expressionism is the Swedish playwright August Strindberg. Twenty-four of his plays were given over a thousand performances in Germany between 1913 and 1915.[6] Like Wedekind, whom he met in Paris, Strindberg perceived that the truth often lies beneath surface reality. After writing a number of more or less conventionally realistic plays, he turned to subjective reality. A well-known example of Strindberg's subjective drama is *A Dream Play* (1907; staged in New York by the Provincetown Players in 1926). Its action is patterned after discontinuous dream formations, and in the preface that could handily serve as a manifesto of dramatic expressionism, Strindberg states his aims.

> As in his previous dream play, *To Damascus*, the author has in *A Dream Play* attempted to reproduce the detached and disunited—although apparently logical—form of dreams. Anything is apt to happen, anything seems possible and probable. Time and space do not exist. On a flimsy foundation of actual happenings, imagination spins and weaves in new patterns: an intermingling of remembrances, experiences, whims, fancies, ideas, fantastic absurdities and

improvisations, and original inventions of the mind. The personalities split, take on duality, multiply, vanish, intensify, diffuse and disperse, and are brought into a focus. There is, however, one singleminded consciousness that exercises a dominance over the characters: the dreamer's.[7]

The essence of this new approach to dramaturgy is easily illustrated by a brief comparison of two plays of different modes that treat similar themes. Both Ibsen's realistic *Ghosts* (1882) and Strindberg's expressionistic *Ghost Sonata* (1908; produced by the Provincetown Players in 1924 as *The Spook Sonata*) comment on the paralyzing effect of what Mrs. Alving in *Ghosts* calls dead ideas and dead beliefs on "the joy of life." Ibsen makes use of discursive language to analyze the stifling effect of social conformity on personal happiness. Strindberg expresses a related idea by means of a grotesque stage metaphor—he creates an obese vampire cook who "boils the life out of the meat," thus symbolically sapping the physical as well as the spiritual and the intellectual strength of the members of the household. In *The Ghost Sonata*, furthermore, the Student is concerned with "the inner life." "What do we find that truly lives up to what it promises?" he asks. The answer is characteristic of the expressionist *Weltanschauung*: "Only things in our dreams, our imagination!"

In addition to the plays of Büchner, Wedekind, and Strindberg, which inspired young German dramatists, new methods of staging and acting helped to bring about the expressionist movement in the theatre. Influenced by the theories of Appia and Craig, as well as by the new mechanical devices for lighting and shifting scenery, such new directors as Max Reinhardt, Leopold Jessner, and Jürgen Fehling altered or eliminated many of the characteristics of the realistic proscenium stage. For painted perspectives and glaring footlights they substituted simplified settings and spotlights. They made use of symbolic, suggestive, and often distorted scenery.

They introduced brilliant colors. And they rediscovered the mask as well as the potential of the human body in creating expressive gestures and rhythms.

In acting, the new approach is best summed up by Paul Kornfeld, who urged the actor not to use the psychological (i.e., the "realistic") method of interpreting a role. Instead, Kornfeld wrote, anticipating Brecht's views on "alienation," the actor should "not be ashamed of the fact that he is acting. Let him not deny the theatre or try to feign reality. . . . Let him therefore pick out the essential attributes of reality and be nothing but a representative of thought, feeling, or fate!" [8] Similarly, the characters in an expressionist play lose their individuality and become types or abstractions not unlike the dramatis personae in medieval morality plays.

One of the first modern German plays in which the characters unmistakably represent abstractions is Oskar Kokoschka's (who is better known as a painter) *Murderer The Women's Hope* (*Mörder Hoffnung der Frauen*, 1908). The action of this thoroughly Dionysiac dream play involving the love-hate relationship of the sexes culminates in a scream. With this scream Kokoschka sounded one of the keynotes of the expressionist movement, for the tense language that echoes Büchner's *Woyzeck* and found pictorial representation in Edvard Munch's angst-ridden painting "The Cry," became the hallmark of much of the new drama.

However, the first expressionist play to receive wide attention was Walter Hasenclever's *The Son* (1916). The work depicts with fresh vigor the age-old conflict between generations, with the action (in twenty-five scenes) presented from the subjective viewpoint of the protagonist. Hasenclever, whose *Beyond* (*Jenseits*, 1920) was produced by the Provincetown Players in 1925, carried the abbreviated language of the expressionists to the point of near absurdity. Much of the action of *Beyond* takes place within the minds of its two characters, a man and a woman, whose love for each other is frustrated by the imagined presence of the woman's dead husband. The grotesquely abbreviated dialogue often consists of spoken thoughts. From time to time the shadow of the husband and other symbolic images materialize on the stage. Time and space are distorted. At the moment of the lovers' death, the walls of the house collapse, the furniture vanishes, and the chandelier floats off into space.

The next landmark in the expressionist theatre was Reinhard Johannes Sorge's *The Beggar* (*Der Bettler,* 1917), a work full of exaggerations. Collective characters (*Gruppenpersonen*), some of whom read aloud from newspapers, stand for the noisy and vulgar everyday world, veiled figures represent projections of the protagonist's mind, and an insane person strikes on a toy drum with a stick that is altogether too big. This kind of exaggeration, frequently approaching the grotesque, became another chief characteristic of German expressionist drama. It is also a prominent feature in expressionist films, of which *The Cabinet of Dr. Caligari* is the most widely known.

Created in Germany in 1919, *Caligari* was released in the United States in the spring of 1921. The work has become a classic of the silent screen and is a splendid example of visual expressionism, for its grotesquely distorted action and settings (painted by three expressionist artists affiliated with the Berlin *Sturm* group) betray the deranged mentality of its protagonist. As we will discover in subsequent chapters, quite a few American experiments in dramaturgy as well as in production are indebted to this single work of Continental expressionism.

While the *Caligari* brand of visual expressionism excited large numbers of American theatre artists, the chief among them, Eugene O'Neill (who learned a great deal from the German film), was also attracted to the plays of Georg Kaiser. Kaiser is generally regarded as the most distinguished of German expressionist playwrights. He was also the most prolific of the German dramatists who wrote during the expressionist period.

In the four years between 1917 and 1920 there were seventeen first nights of his plays. He began as a disciple of Wedekind (and Carl Sternheim) with satires on bourgeois philistinism and then went on to write more than fifty plays of every variety of style and subject matter. Kaiser's work frequently lacks the ecstasy, the *Schrei* quality common to many other expressionist dramas, but it is highly stylized and thoroughly subjective. Despite occasional attempts to disassociate him from the movement, Kaiser's place in expressionism is firmly established.

Of Kaiser's early expressionist plays, the best known in the United States (it was produced by the Theatre Guild in 1922) is *From Morn to Midnight* (*Von Morgens bis Mitternachts*, 1917). It traces through a series of stages, or *Stationen* (a concept which the German expressionists borrowed from Strindberg), the general disillusionment of a bank clerk who tries to buy happiness with embezzled funds. In his search for spiritual fulfillment, he encounters masked abstractions and other one-dimensional types, and speaks in Kaiser's famous "telegram" style. Furthermore, the playwright frequently objectifies the protagonist's unconscious fears. For example, a tree in a snowy field on which the Cashier has been sitting suddenly assumes the form of a grinning skeleton. The illuminated outline of the same projected image appears once more in a chandelier just before the Cashier shoots himself at the end of the play. Kaiser's *Gas* trilogy, a part of which was staged at the Goodman Memorial Theatre in Chicago in 1926, fuses the themes of the father-son conflict, opposition to mechanized civilization, and the regeneration of man with the concept of dual identities in *The Coral* (*Die Koralle*, 1917). In *Gas I* (1918), Kaiser illustrates man's bondage to machines by symbolic distortions. The hand of a worker has grown in size from lifting and depressing the same lever at the factory until the limb has begun to dominate the man. Another's foot, constantly operating a block-switch, has similarly gained control of the entire man. *Gas II* (1920) depicts a nightmare world of military-industrial automatons that is blown up in the total annihilation of mankind.

Another expressionist playwright whose works were performed in the United States and who opposed materialism and militarism was Ernst Toller. His most widely known play is *Man and the Masses* (*Masse-Mensch*). Its original production in 1921 by Jürgen Fehling at the *Volksbühne* in Berlin has become a classic of expressionist stagecraft, as reported by such enthusiastic visitors from the United States as Kenneth Macgowan and Lee Simonson. (The latter staged it for the Theatre Guild in 1924.) On an almost bare stage, dominated by black curtains, platforms, and steps, Fehling and his stage designer Hans Strohbach made brilliant use of spotlights, colors, masks, sound (including music, choral chants, and the rattle of arms), grotesquely distorted stage properties (impossibly high stools and desks), and masses of people. The play traces the passion and the martyrdom of its protagonist in the hands of the brutal capitalistic society and the equally bloodthirsty revolutionary mob. In seven alternating scenes of reality and dream sequences which objectify the protagonist's inner world, Toller analyzes the conflicting ideologies of the individual, the state, and the masses. Toller's later comments on his early plays reveal some of the excitement that the new style offered the young dramatists of his generation and help define an expressionist aesthetic.

> Today many people smile at Expressionism: at that time it was a necessary artistic form. It took a stand against that kind of art which was satisfied with lining up impressions side by side, asking no questions about the essence, the responsibility, the idea. The Expressionist wanted to do more than take photographs. Realizing that the artist's environment, as it were, penetrates him and is reflected in the mirror of his soul, he wanted to recreate this environment in

its very essence. . . . In the Expressionist drama, man was no incidental private person. He was a type, applying to many by leaving out their superficial features. By skinning the human being one hoped to find his soul under the skin.[9]

The innermost soul of man revealed by the new dramaturgy was not always pleasant to contemplate, for in stripping a person of his masks, expressionist playwrights frequently came face to face with the irrational in the human psyche. Thus Franz Werfel, well known in this country as a novelist, explored the Dionysian-Apollonian duality in man (Nietzsche's impact on the expressionist movement must not be underestimated) in such plays as *Mirror-Man* (*Spiegelmensch*, 1921) and *Goat Song* (*Bocksgesang*, 1922). The latter was staged by the Theatre Guild in 1926. A literal translation of the Greek word for tragedy, the title of Werfel's play suggests ancient fertility rites and refers specifically to the agony and ecstasy of the monstrous offspring, part man–part goat, of a Balkan couple. Though the monster is never seen on the stage, he dominates the action of the play and functions as an effective objectification of the Dionysiac in man.

The expressionists' concern with subjective states forced them to fashion dramaturgical techniques that distorted reality and created a nightmarish world of dream images. Actions and objects were no longer viewed photographically but were seen symbolically. Characters ceased to be individuals and became abstractions or types. Dialogue was frequently stripped of all but the essential words or was replaced by appropriate sound effects, including music, the most subjective of the arts. A rapid sequence of scenes, shifting with cinematic speed, formed a series of episodic *Stationen*. These distortions for the sake of objectifying inner truths freed the drama from the rigid conventions of realism and encouraged playwrights to turn to a more imaginative handling of their subject matter. Even though the extremes of presentational drama engendered, soon after 1920, a revival of representational art, called *Neue Sachlichkeit* (literally New Matter-of-Factness or New Objectivity), expressionism continued to play a significant role in the early works of Bertolt Brecht as well as in the plays of such subsequent German-speaking dramatists as Wolfgang Borchert, Friedrich Dürrenmatt, and Peter Weiss.

From Germany a wave of expressionistic productions spread to almost every part of Europe. In the Ukraine, for example, the staging of Kaiser's *Gas* in a Kiev theatre started a controversy that lasted for a year, and the works of Kaiser, Toller, and Hasenclever stirred the theatrical life of the tiny Baltic republic of Estonia. Expressionist plays were being written in Scandinavia (Pär Lagerkvist) and Poland (Stanislaw Ignacy Witkiewicz). In central Europe the new mode left its mark on the playwrights of several countries, notably those of Czechoslovakia (the Čapek brothers). In France, which nurtured Paul Claudel (whose plays may have influenced some of the German writers) and saw the development of Alfred Jarry's subjectivist pataphysics into surrealism, expressionistic techniques influenced the work of such dramatists as Henri-René Lenormand, Jean-Victor Pellerin, Simon Gantillon and a number of more recent playwrights as well as the *mise en scène* of directors Gaston Baty, Georges Pitoëff, and Jean-Louis Barrault. Expressionism can be found also in the plays of the Spanish dramatists Ramón Maria del Valle-Inclán and Federico García Lorca. In Russia the Habima theatre and the Moscow State Jewish Theatre carried on the experimental tradition of Tairov; German expressionist dramas played a significant role in the repertory of Moscow theatres in the twenties; and such Soviet playwrights as Vladimir Mayakovsky and Yurii Olyesha utilized the new technique. In London the Stage Society and the Gate Theatre presented plays by Kaiser, Toller, and Evreinov. Denis Johnston's Irish expressionist drama *The Old Lady Says "No!"* and Sean

O'Casey's *The Silver Tassie* were produced in 1929. It was the expressionistic second act of *The Silver Tassie* that estranged O'Casey and Dublin's Abbey Theatre, which refused to stage the play. After the break the Abbey fell into a decline. O'Casey continued to write nonrealistic plays. "The movement called expressionism," Allardyce Nicoll has said, "would have fully justified its existence even if O'Casey's plays alone were the products of its germinating impulse." [10]

The existence of the movement called expressionism seems even more fully justified when we consider its impact on Eugene O'Neill. The all-American Theatre Creative had indeed cause for alarm. For the development of modern American drama owes much to the European expressionists, whose formal innovations were soon absorbed by several playwrights associated with the Provincetown Players.

2

The Provincetown Players
Jig Cook

In a poem entitled "Provincetown," published in the April 1929 issue of the *Bookman*, Edmund Wilson writes of "the barren beach" and "The desert dropping of a bird,/Bare-bedded in the sandy ground." Though describing a stretch of the Cape Cod coastline, these lines could easily refer to the fertilizing impact of the Provincetown Players on the sandy waste of the American theatrical landscape, where commercialism and Belasco reigned supreme, where realism meant the exact reproduction on the stage of a corner of a Childs Restaurant, and where Broadway, The Great White Way—aptly renamed The Great Trite Way—illuminated a sentimentally artificial and shallow universe.

The public who went to Broadway shows during the first two decades of the twentieth century demanded little more than escape and entertainment. Aside from a few works by William Vaughan Moody and possibly Langdon Mitchell, most native plays presented on Broadway amused the public with superficial comedy, romantic love stories, stereotyped melodrama, or fledgling musicals.

Even the serious drama of the period was hackneyed and melodramatic and firmly tied to a set of extra-aesthetic conventions. The mentality that produced such fare was fully exposed when Augustus Thomas, then the dean of American playwrights, lectured to the students in Professor George Pierce Baker's drama class at Har-

vard on how to write a successful Broadway play.
Thomas began by choosing a popular stage star for
whose talents the play would merely be a vehicle. The
age and physical characteristics of the actress necessi-
tated a work about a mature yet passionate woman.
With a glibness that revolted young Eugene O'Neill, at
that time one of Professor Baker's students, Thomas proceeded to construct a full-length melodrama, whose plot
resembled that of Hawthorne's *The Scarlet Letter*.
When he had finished, Thomas offered to write the
dialogue and guaranteed a production if some member
of the class would write it up as a scenario. Professor
Baker demurred that it was too commercial. O'Neill
went from the classroom directly to Boston and got
drunk.[1] The young playwright's sentiments typify the
attitude of the new generation of artists toward the
commercialism of Broadway. The time was ripe for a
reaction.

There had been sporadic attempts to organize non-
commercial "little theatres" in the United States in the
nineteenth century. One of these, which lasted for three
weeks, was established by James A. Herne in Boston in
1891 for the purpose of staging his *Margaret Fleming*.
Herne's play had been considered too daring in its
realism, and managers had prevented the author from
securing a professional theatre. The American university
has also provided sanctuary for serious art. In 1909 the
Harvard Dramatic Club gave the first performance of
Percy MacKaye's *The Scarecrow*. In this play MacKaye
endeavors to objectify the gap between reality and man's
ideal of human perfection by means of the mirror image
of the protagonist. The conversations between the scarecrow and his reflection in the mirror anticipate later
treatments of the split personality in such works as
O'Neill's *The Great God Brown* and E. E. Cummings's
Him. Though the tone of *The Scarecrow* is hardly that
of expressionism, the general tenor of the MacKaye play
looks forward to the formal experiments in the American drama of the 1920s. Besides other attempts at ex-

perimentation, such as Eleanor Gates's *Poor Little Rich Girl* (1913), Beulah Marie Dix's *Across the Border* (1914), Alice Gerstenberg's *Overtones* (1915), and Owen and Robert H. Davis's *Any House* (1916), a genuine early manifestation of American expressionism is to be found in novelist Theodore Dreiser's *Plays of the Natural and the Supernatural* (published in 1916).

In one of these, called *The Blue Sphere*, characters think aloud, visions of the past materialize on the stage, and the parents' death wish for their deformed baby is given concrete stage reality in the form of the Shadow, which lures the infant to its death under the wheels of a train. Another play in this collection, *In the Dark*, is about a murder and has in its supporting cast a Germanic character named Woitezek. Dreiser's short play *The Dream* (published in his *Hey Rub-a-Dub-Dub*, 1920) presents the distorted figures and landscape of a professor's dream, and there are numerous grotesque objectifications in *Phantasmagoria* (also in *Hey Rub-a-Dub-Dub*). Notwithstanding this seemingly native tradition—MacKaye, however, drew inspiration (misapplied as it was) from Gordon Craig; Dreiser knew Strindberg's *A Dream Play* and may have been acquainted with Büchner's *Woyzeck*—the revolution that swept through the American theatre in the second decade of the twentieth century and gave birth to the modern American drama was European in its sources and its inspiration.

While the cosmopolitan George Jean Nathan blasted "Belascoism" in the pages of *The Smart Set*, William Butler Yeats lectured at Harvard on "The Theatre of Beauty," Winthrop Ames imported Max Reinhardt's musical pantomime *Sumurûn* (1912), New York's German-language Irving Place theatre gave Wedekind's *Spring's Awakening* (1912), Austrian scenic artist Joseph Urban made strikingly unconventional designs for the Boston Opera House, and visitors to the major stage centers of Europe wrote enthusiastically about the new movement in the Continental theatre. Those who had stayed home were startled by the Armory Show of modern European painting, delighted by Diaghilev's Ballets Russes, and intrigued by the new stagecraft of Granville-Barker's productions for the Stage Society, which introduced the brilliant designs of Robert Edmond Jones, a former student of Reinhardt at the *Deutsches Theater* in Berlin. Translations of new European plays began to appear in such periodicals as *The Drama*, sponsored by the Drama League of America, which was founded in 1910 to encourage the production of good drama. And at Harvard, Professor Baker, who had recently returned from Europe, showed his students (among them Eugene O'Neill) lantern slides of the designs of such luminaries of the Continental "new stagecraft" as Adolphe Appia, Gordon Craig, and Ernst Stern, Reinhardt's chief designer. (While in Europe, Baker had met Craig and Reinhardt.) Other professors at other universities brought the literature of Continental drama to the attention of their students. The cause of the new drama and stagecraft was further championed by the *Theatre Arts Magazine*, founded in 1916 to rival the periodical *Theatre*, which supported the theatrical status quo.

The new drama and stagecraft found little encouragement on commercial Broadway. Instead, the new spirit became identified with the little theatre movement, which Belasco called "the cubism of the theater—the wail of the incompetent and the degenerate." [2] Influenced, no doubt, by the example of such European groups as Antoine's *Théâtre Libre* in Paris, *Die Freie Bühne* in Berlin, J. T. Grein's The Independent Theatre in London, and Stanislavsky's The Moscow Art Theatre, the beginnings of the American little theatre movement go back to 1906–7, when Victor Mapes, Donald Robertson, and Laura Dainty Pelham launched productions of new plays in Chicago. In 1912, inspired by the recent visit of the Irish Players of Dublin's Abbey Theatre, Mrs. Lyman W. Gale founded the Toy Theatre in Boston. Shortly thereafter, Maurice Browne opened The Little Theatre in Chicago. In New York, Winthrop Ames, who had recently directed the repertory at the ill-fated New Theatre, established his Little Theatre, and Holbrook Blinn launched the Princess Players, for whose stage Clayton Hamilton, in the only review of Eugene O'Neill's *Thirst* volume of one-act dramas (*Bookman*, April 1915), recommended "more than one of these plays." A more permanent impression on the American drama was made in 1915 with the opening of The Neighborhood Playhouse, the first season of the Washington Square Players (who later became the influential Theatre Guild) at the Bandbox Theatre, and the founding of the Provincetown Players.

The story of the Provincetown Players has been recorded by several hands. It began in the summer of 1915 when a party of Greenwich Village writers and artists, some of whom had participated in the birth of the Washington Square Players, gathered in Provincetown, Massachusetts, and entertained themselves by putting on their own plays. One of the reasons why George Cram ("Jig") Cook, who emerged as the leader of the new group, had felt uncomfortable with the Washington Square Players was that the latter produced mainly European experimentalists. Cook's aim was "to give American playwrights a chance to work out their ideas in freedom." The Players' theory of acting, if they bothered at all to expound one, held no room for the exaggerated dramatics of the commercial theatre. When the celebrated actor James O'Neill was asked to help the Players direct his son's *Before Breakfast*, the younger O'Neill "stalked up and down, muttering his displeasure" at his father's attempt to lecture an actress on "the histrionic technique of an era which the Players had no wish to revive." The Players' methods of staging were subject to the limitations of their purse. And economic considerations—their most expensive set cost thirteen dollars—prohibited extensive experimentation with scenic styles. In staging O'Neill's *Thirst*, for example, William Zorach, who had designed abstract settings for

Louise Bryant's morality play *The Game*, wanted to make a backdrop of formalized waves but was prevented by Cook, who insisted that O'Neill was a realistic playwright.[3] O'Neill chafed under these restrictions and undoubtedly helped to persuade Cook to invest in updating the tiny Provincetown stage. As a result, for the 1920 première of O'Neill's *The Emperor Jones*, the Provincetown Players, who had meanwhile settled in a converted stable in New York's Greenwich Village, installed a device of the new stagecraft—the sky-dome, or *Kuppel-horizont*, as the Germans called it.

That the original Provincetown Players tended to lean toward realism is suggested also by the reminiscences of Alfred Kreymborg, who joined the group during its first season and whose *Lima Beans* the Players produced on December 1, 1916, with William Carlos Williams in the cast. "We're strong on realism and weak on fantasy," confessed Zorach to Kreymborg. "Maybe you can supply the latter." [4] Kreymborg did. *Lima Beans* is in many ways typical of his Craigian puppet-plays. There is considerable pantomime, a strong ritualistic element pervades the work, and the dialogue is not only lyrical but greatly abbreviated and disconnected. There is an attempt, furthermore, at visual communication of verbal rhythms.

His next play, *Manikin and Minikin*, involving two porcelain figurines on a mantlepiece, who talk to the metronomic accompaniment of the clock that stands between them, was rejected by the Provincetown Players. Kreymborg was not to be denied, however. With Zorach, Edna St. Vincent Millay, and other sympathizers, he founded The Other Players and staged *Manikin and Minikin* as well as his *Jack's House* as an independent production on the Provincetown stage on March 18, 1918. *Jack's House* contains several touches of expressionistic distortion and objectification. When the curtain, which depicts "a fantastic cartoon" of geometric designs, lifts, Jack is revealed sitting in a large chair behind a small desk, wearing "Large square-rimmed spectacles" and studying "a ponderous volume across which may be read the words, HOUSEHOLD ACCOUNTS." Jack's subjective preoccupation with household arithmetic and his thoughts formed by association are objectified when he recites, while gesticulating "geometrically,"

> Two and two are four,
> four and six are ten,
> ten and two are twelve,
> twelve and nine are twenty-one—
> twenty-one—
> Wife is only twenty—
> twenty-one—
> twenty-one and seven—
> oh how I hope—
> twenty-one and seven—
> twenty-nine—
> oh how I hope—
> carry two—
> I hope she'll do the housework soon.[5]

Jack's House was published along with *Lima Beans* and *Manikin and Minikin* in 1918 in a volume Kreymborg titled *Plays for Poem-Mimes*. Of the other plays in this collection, *Blue and Green* and *People Who Die* offer further examples of Kreymborg's mildly expressionistic dramaturgy. The latter is subtitled *A Dream-Play* and involves a man and a woman sitting on a bench in front of the curtain. He talks of writing a play about death. As the curtains part several times during the course of the play, characters appear, representing the couple on the bench at various moments in the past. The play ends with the couple's falling asleep. Their yearning for each other and their departed love are objectified by means of two shadows who "speak in lively echo-whispers" (p. 125). *Blue and Green*, subtitled *A Shadow-Play*, speaks of the transitoriness of life and the selfishness and fragility of love. When the lovers meet some time later, Kreymborg concretizes their "lost love." "Two shadows take entity among the live oaks" (p. 75).

They dance a dirge and pantomime segments of the lovers' first meeting. When the lovers leave together, toward the "you" in each, the shadows "dance an ethereal movement, suggesting an apotheosis of [that] motive" (p. 84).

On February 13, 1920, the Provincetown Players produced Kreymborg's *Vote the New Moon*. It depicts the conflict between the Blue and Red forces, both seeking to achieve for their candidates the mayorality of a town. The characters in this one-act political satire look like jacks-in-the-box; the candidates engage in ritualistic posturing and movement; the voting is done by a representative Burgher and Burgess, who smite each other on the head with hammers until one or the other is insensible; and the language is abbreviated and rhythmic, as in the following speeches that reinforce the rapping of the voters' hammers:

CRIER —   What do you mean?
BURGHER —   We mean—
BURGESS —   We're tired—
CRIER —   Tired?
BURGHER —   Of old moons—
BURGESS —   We want—
CRIER —   You want?
DUO —   A new moon![6]

Eventually both sides join in denouncing the local sovereign, who thereupon rises from the river ("a huge, misshapen figure"), swallows all except the Town Crier, (who looks like a scarecrow), and slouches toward the town hall to become the new burgomaster. By means of exaggerated characters, grotesquely distorted action, and staccato language—tools of the expressionist playwright —Kreymborg has succeeded in objectifying archetypal political struggle and tyranny.

Kreymborg matured in the company of experimental artists, found himself ostracized for his "persistent predilection for 'these moderns'," [7] and edited such little magazines as the *Glebe*, which published, in addition to

Ezra Pound's *Des Imagistes*, translations of Wedekind's
and Andreyev's plays. It is only natural then that his
dramatic experiments should reflect the formal innovations associated with European expressionism. As
Moody E. Prior has pointed out in his study *The Language of Tragedy*, Kreymborg's early work is in the tradition of expressionistic verse drama and should be
taken seriously. One does not, of course, have to agree
with Waldo Frank that Kreymborg has more claim to
be called a founder of the modern American theatre
than Eugene O'Neill.[8] Nevertheless, Kreymborg deserves
to be recognized as an imaginative formal innovator.

Unlike Kreymborg's predominantly experimental
early work, O'Neill's first plays tend to be realistic. An
exception is *Fog*. In this short drama, written in 1913–14,
soon after O'Neill had spent considerable time reading
the Greeks, the Elizabethans, Strindberg, and other
moderns, the young playwright shows a predilection for
symbols, type characters, and an imaginative use of
sound. The play deals with a group of shipwrecked people—a Poet, a Business Man, a Peasant Woman, and her
Dead Child—adrift in a boat which has come to rest on
an iceberg that is hidden from sight by a bank of fog.
The Business Man wants to call to a passing ship for
help, but the Poet, fearing that the steamer might wreck
itself on the fog-shrouded iceberg, prevents him. When
it is revealed at the end of the play that a rescue party
has been led to the boat by the voice of the Dead Child,
an unreal, dreamlike atmosphere pervades the work,
foreshadowing O'Neill's later expressionist plays.

Fog was staged by the Provincetown Players in January of 1917. The first O'Neill work to be produced by
the Players was *Bound East for Cardiff* (summer of
1916). In 1935 O'Neill referred to it as "very important
from my point of view. In it can be seen, or felt, the
germ of the spirit, life-attitude, etc., of all my more important future work."[9] *Bound East for Cardiff* tells the
relatively actionless story of a sailor's death at sea. The
handling of the situation is basically realistic, but

O'Neill is unable to keep the expressionistic "higher re-ality" from invading the stage in the scene where Yank, the dying sailor, stares with horror at "a pretty lady dressed in black," [10] a figure that exists only in his deliri-ous imagination.

In *Bound East for Cardiff* no one except Yank sees the lady in black. In *Where the Cross Is Made*, however, O'Neill objectifies a subjective vision. Produced by the Provincetown Players on November 22, 1918, *Where the Cross Is Made* is about an old sea captain who refuses to accept reality. He and his companions have buried two chests of worthless native ornaments on a desert island. Believing the trinkets to be a treasure, they have marked the spot on their map with a cross. The old captain also knows, but refuses to believe, that the ship that sailed to recover the "treasure" has been lost in a storm. The play is characterized by tense and disjointed speech, and when the mad captain succeeds in persuading his son to share his wild dreams, O'Neill objectifies the diseased state of their minds. On the stage appear the grotesque forms of the captain's three companions who drowned when their ship went down.

> *The forms . . . rise noiselessly into the room from the stairs. . . . All are in their bare feet. Water drips from their soaked and rotten clothes. Their hair is matted, intertwined with slimy strands of seaweed. Their eyes, as they glide silently into the room, stare frightfully wide at nothing. Their flesh in the green light has the suggestion of decomposition. Their bod-ies sway limply, nervelessly, rhythmically as if to the pulse of long swells of the deep sea.* [1, 571]

When the play was being rehearsed by the Province-town Players and some members of the group wanted to eliminate the ghosts, O'Neill insisted that the scene be played as he wrote it. He told the Players that his intent was to "hypnotize the audience so when they see the ghosts they will think they are mad too!" [11] What he was really doing was giving concrete dramatic form to the inner reality of his protagonist.

Another of O'Neill's contemporaries, aside from Alfred Kreymborg, whose plays were staged by the Provincetown Players and who seems to have been aware of
the formal experiments of the expressionists was Jig
Cook's wife, Susan Glaspell. Though her other plays are
conventionally realistic, *The Verge*, which the Players
produced on November 14, 1921, deals imaginatively
with a woman who eventually loses her mind. The most
obvious expressionistic device in the play is the distorted
setting of act 2, which depicts Claire's mental state; the
tower *"is thought to be round but does not complete the
circle. The back is curved, then jagged lines break from
that, and the front is a queer bulging window—in a curve
that leans. The whole structure is as if given a twist by
some terrific force—like something wrung."* [12] The light
escaping through the slits in a metal lantern throws a
grotesque pattern on the curved wall and constitutes the
visual image of Claire's concept of gayety: "Here is the
circle we are in. [*Describes a big circle.*] Being gay. It
shoots little darts through the circle, and a minute later
—gayety all gone, and you looking through that little
hole the gayety left" (pp. 66–67). That the playwright is
here objectifying the protagonist's inner state becomes
apparent when Claire addresses her sister in words that
find their counterpart in the stage setting: "But never
one of you—once—looked with me through the little
pricks the gayety made—never one of you—once, looked
with me at the queer light that came in through the
pricks" (p. 67). Similarly, the distorted rail of the spiral
staircase, the names of the flowers Claire grows—e.g.,
Breath of Life, Edge Vine—and her tense and disjointed
language, especially toward the end of the play, suggest
both a view into the disturbed mind of the protagonist
as well as an approximation of how reality must appear
to a person on the verge of insanity.

Cleon Throckmorton's design for the second act of
The Verge captured the subjectively distorted appearance of the tower room and reminded Kenneth Macgowan, who reviewed Miss Glaspell's play in the *New
York Globe* (November 15, 1921), of something out of

The Cabinet of Dr. Caligari. In one of the first applications of the term to a New York production (the same critic had several weeks earlier spoken of expressionist/cubist stagecraft in Philadelphia and Chicago), Macgowan called Throckmorton's scenic approach in *The Verge* "expressionistic."

Notwithstanding the expressionistic second act of Susan Glaspell's *The Verge* as well as the introduction of a strong element of fantasy and stylization into such works as Louise Bryant's *The Game,* James Oppenheim's *Night,* Maxwell Bodenheim's *The Gentle Furniture Shop,* Edna St. Vincent Millay's *Aria da Capo,* Cloyd Head's *Grotesques,* and Pierre Loving's *The Stick-Up,* most plays staged by the Provincetown Players under Jig Cook's leadership were realistic. Even *The Verge* and O'Neill's *Where the Cross Is Made* are basically realistic works. The scenes of expressionistic objectification in these plays appear to be a mere groping toward the new form. Nevertheless, they clearly indicate the direction the work of the playwrights associated with the Provincetown Players was soon to take. Alfred Kreymborg's *Jack's House* and *Vote the New Moon* are thoroughly experimental, but their production left no mark on the theatrical life of the day. An early experimental Provincetown play that generated a great deal of excitement, however, and fertilized not only the sterile theatrical landscape of Broadway but the development of modern American drama in general was O'Neill's *The Emperor Jones.*

3

Eugene O'Neill

When Bertolt Brecht told a Danish interviewer in 1934
that "People like Georg Kaiser and his follower O'Neill
have successfully applied quite new methods which are
good and interesting even if their ideas don't coincide
with my own," he had obviously not heard about
O'Neill's protestations that he "did not think much" of
Kaiser's plays, because they were "too easy" and "would
not have influenced" him.[1] Despite his disavowals of
Kaiser's influence, O'Neill's attempts to objectify inner
experiences by means of the forms of a stylized theatre
have much in common with the techniques of the Continental expressionists. Most American critics, however,
took O'Neill's remarks at face value and dismissed the
possibility of his affinity with the German expressionists
by merely quoting his denials. The adjective "expressionistic" has, of course, been applied to several of
O'Neill's plays, but the tendency has been to minimize
his ties with the Germans and to emphasize his indebtedness to Strindberg. O'Neill's Nobel Prize address, in
which he named the Swedish playwright as his chief
mentor, has reinforced this point of view. Undeniably,
O'Neill's work owes a debt to August Strindberg. Yet
failure to account for the influence of the German expressionists in general and Georg Kaiser in particular
makes it difficult to evaluate O'Neill's development as
an experimenter with dramatic form.

O'Neill's initial acquaintance with the new movement

in the German theatre may date back to his one year (1914–15) at Harvard as a member of George Pierce Baker's course in playwriting. Professor Baker had recently returned from Europe and spoke highly of the new Continental theatres, observing that "Germany is far ahead of us in successful stage devices." [2] O'Neill did not find the academic atmosphere favorable for creative work, but during his stay in Cambridge he began to learn German in order to read Nietzsche and Wedekind in the original.[3] By the time he had spent a couple of seasons with the Provincetown Players, whom he joined in 1916, he had acquired a considerable familiarity with the new Continental drama. In the August 1921 issue of the *Bookman,* Pierre Loving describes a meeting with O'Neill that had taken place several years before in a New York bar. Loving and a woman novelist were "talking about several foreign dramatists whose works were not yet familiar to the American public" when they were interrupted by O'Neill, who "launched into a brilliant analysis" of the dramatists whom Loving and his lady friend had been discussing. O'Neill then told the group that "he had just read the newer men in their original tongue." Loving, whose own survey of German expressionist drama was published in 1925,[4] does not specify the nationalities of the dramatists under discussion, but Mary Heaton Vorse, in whose fish house on a Provincetown wharf the Players staged O'Neill's first play, is more explicit in her recollections. She remembers discussing the new German playwrights with O'Neill and other members of the Provincetown group after she returned from Europe in 1919. During this trip Miss Vorse had been greatly impressed by what she had seen in the European theatres, and she had met Ernst Toller.[5] In June of 1920, shortly before writing *The Emperor Jones,* O'Neill himself admitted in a letter to George Jean Nathan that he was "familiar enough with the best modern drama of all countries." [6] That O'Neill was acquainted specifically with modern German drama is suggested by his wife's comments in an article she pub-

lished in 1924. While noting that the great experimentalists in the theatre were Strindberg, Ibsen, Wedekind,
and Kaiser, she warned young artists not to forgo their
own individuality by imitating earlier successful experiments, such as *Ulysses*, the work of Picasso, or German
expressionism.[7]

As Clara Blackburn suggested in her 1941 *American
Literature* article, "Continental Influences on Eugene
O'Neill's Expressionistic Dramas," the fable and the
form of *The Emperor Jones* resemble Georg Kaiser's
From Morn to Midnight, which O'Neill said he had read
before it was produced in New York in 1922, but which,
he insisted, had not influenced him. In Kaiser's play the
seven relatively short scenes are held together by the figure of the Cashier who has embezzled bank funds.
Through the monologues and the dizzy wanderings of
this allegorical character who, like Jones, is in flight as
the result of his greed, Kaiser presents the action of the
play as seen through the eyes of the protagonist. The
skeleton in the tree, the identically dressed gentlemen at
the bicycle races, the masked prostitutes in the cabaret
scene, and the Salvation Army penitents whose confes-
sions reveal uncanny similarities with the Cashier's own
situation, are emanations from his unconscious mind,
not unlike the visions of Brutus Jones. For the forest
through which Jones must pass in order to reach safety is
a jungle not only of physical trees but also of mental images, ranging from the Little Formless Fears, an expressionistic objectification of his guilty conscience, which
"creep out from the deeper blackness of the forest," [8]
i.e., from the inner recesses of his unconscious mind, to
the crocodile god who rules over O'Neill's version of the
heart of darkness.

These points of likeness between *The Emperor Jones*
and *From Morn to Midnight* suggest the possibility that
O'Neill may have been introduced to Kaiser's works by
some acquaintance who, like Mary Heaton Vorse, or
Robert Edmond Jones, or Kenneth Macgowan, returned
from Germany full of enthusiasm for Continental drama

and stagecraft. In the case of *From Morn to Midnight*, however, there was no need to read the German text. Ashley Dukes's version of this work, the first German play to be translated into English after the war, was published in England in May of 1920. In the fall of that year, when O'Neill was working on *The Emperor Jones* (the MS in the Princeton University Library is dated October 2, 1920), the same translation appeared in this country in the journal *Poet Lore*.

When *The Emperor Jones* was produced in Berlin in 1924—its tumultuous New York première took place at the Provincetown Playhouse on November 3, 1920—reviewers were annoyed at the idea of importing such a play, for "expressionistic distortions of emotion were prevalent enough in Germany." Critic Felix Emmel, however, devoted a section of his book on the "ecstatic theatre" to *The Emperor Jones* and praised it with expressionistic vigor: "Here is the breath of theatre. The power of drama. Intimate contact with tragedy. . . . At last a play." [9] O'Neill himself revealed his expressionist orientation in a letter to Harry Weinberger (January 26, 1922; MS in the Eugene O'Neill Collection, Collection of American Literature, Yale University Library; hereafter cited as the Yale Library). Replying to Weinberger's query about the possibility of filming the play, O'Neill stated that the movie rights to *Jones* were not open at present and added by way of explanation, "I am working out a scheme for its filming along Expressionistic lines with the husband of my aunt-in-law—an Italian who worked for years as director of one of their biggest film companies over there. He has done some remarkable work in Italy along the line that I would like to have 'Jones' developed for the screen."

Nothing came of this project (a film version of *Jones* was released by United Artists in 1933), but O'Neill continued with the expressionist mode in *The Hairy Ape*, in which he again objectifies the inner experience of the protagonist. The opening scene of this play develops the cage image from the first scene of *From Morn to Midnight* and requires a setting that mirrors the distorted mental state of Yank. "*The treatment of this scene*," writes O'Neill in the stage directions,

> *or of any other scene in the play, should by no means be naturalistic. The effect sought after is a cramped space in the bowels of a ship, imprisoned by white steel. The lines of bunks, the uprights supporting them, cross each other like the steel framework of a cage. The ceiling crushes down upon the men's heads. They cannot stand upright. This accentuates the natural stooping posture which shoveling coal and the resultant over-development of back and shoulder muscles have given them. The men themselves should resemble those pictures in which the appearance of Neanderthal Man is guessed at.* [P. 207]

By specifying that the setting of the play "should by no means be naturalistic," O'Neill had probably in mind the stage techniques of the Continental expressionists, for in a letter to Nathan the playwright expressed hope that Robert Edmond Jones would do "the eight sets, which must be in the Expressionistic method." [10]

O'Neill's use of nightmarish sight and sound effects in the stokehole and the creation of a subjectively distorted jeweler's window on Fifth Avenue (reminiscent of a scene in Kaiser's *Hell, Road, Earth* [*Hölle Weg Erde*, 1919]) have been singled out as examples of his expressionistic dramaturgy. We might add that O'Neill characterizes the crowd on Fifth Avenue as "a procession of gaudy marionettes" (p. 236) and that though his stage directions do not call for masks, he resorted to the use of this device in the original Provincetown production of the play in order to indicate the "identically haughty and vacant" faces of the people on the street. [11] At the end of this scene O'Neill objectifies in concrete, visual terms Yank's inner thoughts and portrays with symbolic action the outsider's impotent attacks on organized society. Yank screams at the women, but "they seem neither to see nor hear him." He tries to jostle the

men, but he does not jar them; "rather it is he who re-
coils after each collison." He drives his fist into a "fat
gentleman's face. But the gentleman stands unmoved as
if nothing had happened." Finally the fat gentleman announces that Yank's antics have made him lose his bus,
and he calls for a policeman. In typically expressionist
fashion, "a whole platoon of policemen rush in" and
subdue Yank. "The crowd at the window," continues
O'Neill, "have not moved or noticed this disturbance.
The clanging gong of the patrol wagon approaches with
a clamoring din" (pp. 238–39).

The other scenes of this play are less obviously distorted, but when the time came for *The Hairy Ape* to
be made into a movie, O'Neill suggested that an expressionistic scene be added to the script. "Yank, after his
frustrated I.W.W. experiences," wrote O'Neill to Robert F. Sisk (March 21, 1935; MS in the Yale Library),
"resolves he'll blow up steel all on his own. So, with this
idea in mind, he gets a job in the Nazareth works and
you see him there working for steel. He steals dynamite
and sets it off. But again, a fiasco and frustration. All his
attempt does is to blow down a section of wall—and immediately an army of workers rebuilds the wall up before his eyes (an expressionistic touch)."

In addition to certain echoes from *From Morn to
Midnight* and *Hell, Road, Earth,* parallels can be drawn
between *The Hairy Ape* and several other plays by
Kaiser. Yank's identification with steel at the beginning
of the play, for example, can be compared to the scene
in Kaiser's *Gas,* Part I, in which a workman's hand and
another's foot, constantly making the same movement,
have come to dominate the machine-controlled bodies
and souls of these men. And as in *The Hairy Ape,* a key
scene in Kaiser's *The Coral* contrasts the idle rich on
board a vessel with the toiling stokers who suffer below
deck. There is a further similarity between Mildred and
the Billionaire's Daughter from *The Coral,* whose knowl-
edge of ships is confined to the upper deck; and her
brother, in a speech that reveals Kaiser's social conscience, gives a preview of O'Neill's play.

And the vividest picture of all is the "Freedom of the Seas" as she lay in her wharf. Flags, music, passengers in light clothes strolling up and down the decks, chattering, gay. And a few yards underneath their feet, hell. Men feeding fire-belching holes, quivering bodies burning to death. So that we may make speed, speed. . . . Look at us lying back in these chairs in indolence, wailing about the heat the sun pours down on us. We sip iced water for ease, and not a grain of dust irritates our throats. And underneath the soft soles of your white shoes here, there are men with boiling fever in their veins. Tear away this wall of wooden planks—see how thin it is, but yet how fearfully it divides—and look down, look down, all of you! [12]

O'Neill's frequent use of rapidly moving short scenes, a device also employed by Kaiser, has been compared to the technique of the motion picture. Thus Clifford Leech suggests that O'Neill's work in *The Emperor Jones* and *The Hairy Ape* "should be seen in relation to S. M. Eisenstein's films *Battleship Potemkin* (1925) and *October* (1928)." [13] Both of these films postdate *The Hairy Ape*. The basic principles underlying the form of *The Hairy Ape* may, however, be more profitably compared to those employed in the German expressionist film *The Cabinet of Dr. Caligari*.

The action of *Caligari* reflects the workings of the insane mind of the protagonist. As a consequence, visual aspects of the film are correspondingly distorted. These include houses that are askew, windows in the shape of rhombuses, grotesquely tilted streetlights, and frequent use of diagonals, reminding one of O'Neill's description of the forecastle, the exaggerated jeweler's window on Fifth Avenue, and his use of a diagonal row of prison cells in scene six. The frail-looking heroine of the film is dressed in white to provide contrast with the sable garments of her abductor. Indeed, *Caligari* is filled with juxtaposed areas of light and darkness. *The Hairy Ape* offers similar contrasts. Whenever, for example, a furnace door is opened, the shadowy stokehole is illuminated by a flash of intense light. Mildred, whom O'Neill describes as "a white apparition" (p. 225), is contrasted with the stokers, who are covered with black coal dust. The German film contains a scene in a prison cell, with light throwing a grotesque, geometrical pattern upon the crazily leaning walls. A prisoner, ironed to a huge chain and ball, sits in his cell in a sculptured pose. It is not inconceivable that O'Neill's lighting arrangements and his use of the *"Penseur"* motif were suggested by this expressionist film, for O'Neill saw *The Cabinet of Dr. Caligari* in the summer of 1921. Soon afterward he communicated to a friend his enthusiastic reaction: "I saw 'Caligari' and it sure opened my eyes to wonderful possibilities I had never dreamed of before." Six months later he quickly recast a now lost short story that contained the germ idea of *The Hairy Ape* in the form of a play characterized by expressionistic distortions.[14]

When *The Hairy Ape* opened at the Provincetown Playhouse on March 9, 1922, not many reviewers recognized its formal innovations. Kenneth Macgowan, however, hailed it as America's first expressionist drama (*Theatre Arts*, July 1922), a battle raged in the pages of the *Freeman* over the expressionism in the play, and Brock Pemberton, who had recently returned from a trip to Germany (*New York Globe*, April 15, 1922), compared O'Neill's play with the German expressionist works he had seen in Berlin. Similarly, the visiting German critic Alfred Kerr (*New York Times*, May 14, 1922) found in O'Neill's method an "old acquaintance, Sir Expressionism." Kerr also pointed out that Robert Edmond Jones, who had designed the play with Cleon Throckmorton, had unmistakably been influenced by the Berlin production of Toller's *Masse-Mensch*. Jones's enthusiasm for the new stagecraft must have been shared by his codesigner, for Throckmorton, like O'Neill, is on record as an admirer of *The Cabinet of Dr. Caligari.*[15] O'Neill himself described *The Hairy Ape* in a letter to Kenneth Macgowan (December 24, 1921; MS in the Yale Library) as seeming to "run the whole gamut from extreme naturalism to extreme expressionism – with more of the latter than the former." In an interview published in the *American Magazine* (November 1922), O'Neill stated that the key to the understanding of *The Hairy Ape* was the fact that "the whole play is expressionistic." In a *New York Herald Tribune* interview (November 16, 1924), he said that "the real contribution of the expressionist has been in the dynamic qualities of his plays," for O'Neill felt that these works "expressed something in modern life better than did the old plays." Then he added, "I have something of this method in 'The Hairy Ape.' "

Something of this method appears also in *The Great God Brown*, which was produced at the Greenwich Village Theatre on January 23, 1926. In his manuscript foreword to the play, O'Neill calls realism "insufficient" for portraying the inner life of man. Like the German expressionist theoretician Kasimir Edschmid, for whom facts had meaning only so long as the artist penetrated them in order to grasp that which lies beyond, O'Neill felt that "the theatre should be a refuge from the facts of life which . . . have nothing to do with the truth." The theatre, said O'Neill, should lift us to a plane beyond realism and drive us "deep into the unknown within and behind ourselves." [16]

The Great God Brown is a probing into that beyond. Reduced to its simplest outline, the action of this play involves the traditional triangle, which seems at first, however, to have four sides. Dion Anthony, a sensitive artist, is married to Margaret, who loves her husband but is unable to share his inner life. Only Cybel, the "full-breasted and wide-hipped" whore, who "chews gum like a sacred cow" (p. 278), understands him. Dion's rival with both women is his friend and employer William Brown, a successful but hollow materialist. Upon Dion's death, Brown assumes his friend's identity, hoping thereby to acquire Dion's artistic talent and his success with women. This transfer of personality is accomplished with masks.

When the play begins, Dion wears the mask of "a mocking, reckless, defiant, gayly scoffing and sensual young Pan" in an effort to hide a "passionately super-sensitive" face (p. 260). Margaret is masked with "an exact, almost transparent reproduction of her own features," which gives her "the abstract quality of a Girl instead of the individual" (p. 262). Her inability to see beneath the deceiving exterior of Dion is revealed in the scenes in which she refuses to recognize Dion until he has put on his mask. Cybel, on the other hand, who wears a "rouged and eye-blackened" mask of a "hardened prostitute" (p. 279), succeeds in penetrating into the inner reality of Dion. In her presence he removes his mask. Brown remains unmasked until Dion's death. As the action of the play progresses, Dion's face remains that of "an ascetic, a martyr, furrowed by pain and self-torture, yet lighted from within by a spiritual calm and human kindliness" (p. 284). His mask, however, becomes ravaged (not unlike the portrait of Dorian Gray in Oscar Wilde's novel), changing into "diabolical Mephistophelean cruelty and irony" (p. 285). With Brown the process is reversed. When he starts wearing his mask, it is an "exact likeness of his face—the self-assured success" (p. 303). While his mask remains unchanged, Brown's face becomes "tortured and distorted by the demon of Dion's mask" (p. 305). When Billy Brown puts on his friend's mask, it appears as if Dion and Brown were really the two warring personae of one individual, with Dion's death symbolizing the triumph of the dominating half of the Dion-Brown personality over the weaker one. For O'Neill was a skilled enough craftsman not to have killed off his protagonist halfway through the play—after a long conflict, artistic and spiritual values (Dion) expire in the embrace of materialism (Brown), making the seemingly four-sided structure a triangle after all.

That Dion Anthony and Billy Brown are merely expressionistic objectifications of a multiple personality (anticipating the more obviously presented split between John, the believer, and Loving, the atheist, in O'Neill's

Days Without End) is suggested on several levels throughout the play. Like Edgar Allan Poe's William Wilson and his alter ego, Dion and Brown are of the same age, same height, shared the same room in college, and studied for the same profession. Interrupting Dion and Cybel in act 1, scene 3, Brown seems to act as Dion's conscience, trying to get Dion to leave Cybel's room. Later, when Dion accuses Brown of attempting to steal his "love of the flesh" just as he is stealing Dion's ideas, Cybel suggests that they are "brothers, I guess, somehow" (p. 287). Posing as Dion in act 4, Brown says to Margaret, who comments on the likeness of their suits, "We're getting to be like twins" (p. 316). When the dying Dion demands a drink, Brown says, "All right. It's your funeral." Dion replies, "And William Brown's! When I die, he goes to hell!" (p. 295). When Dion and Brown stare at each other just before Dion announces his "last will and testament," leaving "Dion Anthony to William Brown," Dion says to Brown, "Ah! Now he looks into the mirror! Now he sees his face!" (p. 298). Dion's last sentence, " 'Our Father.' . . . ," is completed by Brown at the moment of his death: "Who art!" And when he realizes that Margaret will always love Dion, Brown says, "You're dead, William Brown. . . . It's the Dion you buried in your garden who killed you, not you him!" (p. 305). Similarly, Brown points to the mask of Dion in the last act and says, "I am his murderer and his murdered!" (p. 320). These sentences are somewhat puzzling, because Brown did not physically kill Dion. They begin to make sense, however, when we look at the death of Dion as the triumph of the materialistic half of the Dion-Brown personality over the artistic one. This interpretation is reinforced by Cybel's referring to Billy Brown as "*Dion* Brown" (p. 320; my italics). That Dion and Brown are an expressionistic objectification of a multiple personality is further suggested by the text of a telegram O'Neill addressed to actor John Barrymore, asking him to play the lead: "Am taking liberty send you my latest play The Great God Brown thinking may interest you as vehicle. Dion in first half and Brown in rest of play should be played by same actor but you alone could do this. . . ." [17]

The genesis of Dion-Brown's dual personality may go back to O'Neill's reading of Oscar Wilde's *The Picture of Dorian Gray*, Euripides' *The Bacchae*, or even Nietzsche's *The Birth of Tragedy*. The expressionistic dramatization of the split personality suggests, however, the influence of Leonid Andreyev's *The Black Maskers*, which appeared in an English translation in 1925 when O'Neill was writing *The Great God Brown*. In the Andreyev play the protagonist's thoughts are objectified by means of masked characters, and the hero is killed halfway through the play in a duel with his alter ego. Yet *The Great God Brown* has an affinity also with Georg Kaiser's *The Coral*. In Kaiser's play the Billionaire murders his Secretary (who is, in fact, his alter ego), assumes the dead man's identity in an effort to obtain the victim's peace of mind, is mistaken for his murdered subordinate, and is executed for having murdered himself, as it were. This is precisely what happens in *The Great God Brown*. In O'Neill's play Brown, who wants to acquire his rival's identity, begins to wear Dion's mask upon the latter's death. Posing as Dion, he soon casts off ("kills") his own mask (his real self) and is shot by the police—who mistake him for Dion—for murdering Brown (i.e., himself). Kaiser's characters have identical physical features; the only distinguishing characteristic is a small piece of red coral worn by the Secretary on his watch chain. O'Neill handles the change in personality with the skillful use of masks.

Of the many critics who have commented on O'Neill's use of masks in *The Great God Brown*, Stark Young is perhaps the most penetrating. Writing in the *New Republic* (February 10, 1926), Young finds the masks both economical and meaningful in terms of artistic expression. "Coming on and off [the faces] as they do when these human beings confront one another," he wrote in his review of the play, the masks "say quickly and clearly certain things that need to be said," as at the very end of the play when Margaret talks "to the mask of the dead man whom she has loved but never known as he was, folding him now like a child in the bosom of her love." Here Young captures the essence of what O'Neill was trying to communicate with masks, for, he goes on to say, when we "realize that it is still only his mask that she kneels to there, the motive becomes suddenly luminous and revealing." It is in the visual presentation of subjective reality—in this case Margaret's failure to understand her husband, her inability to see beyond his external persona—that O'Neill's use of masks may be called expressionistic.

O'Neill's own views on the mask were published in the November 1932 issue of the *American Spectator* in an essay entitled "Memoranda on Masks." In it he states that "the use of masks will be discovered eventually to be the freest solution of the modern dramatist's problem as to how—with the greatest possible dramatic clarity and economy of means—he can express those profound hidden conflicts of the mind which the probings of psychology continue to disclose to us." For what, asked O'Neill, is "the new psychological insight into human cause and effect but a study in masks, an exercise in unmasking?" He concluded that "this insight has uncovered the mask, has impressed the idea of mask as a symbol of inner reality upon all intelligent people of today." The series of essays that O'Neill wrote for the *American Spectator* (reprinted in Cargill, *O'Neill and His Plays*), of which "Memoranda on Masks" is the first, reveals his affinity with the German expressionists, for in these essays he speaks of "a non-realistic imaginative theatre" in terms of "inner drama," "a drama of souls," and "inner reality." One method in objectifying the states of the ego was to use masks, as does Kaiser, for example, in *From Morn to Midnight*. O'Neill's essay on the mask brings to mind, furthermore, the German expressionists' theories concerning this device. "We have forgotten entirely that the primary symbol of the theatre is the mask," wrote playwright Yvan Goll. "In the mask lies a law, and this is the law of the drama. Non-reality becomes fact." And in the words of Lothar Schreyer, one of the *Sturm* expressionists, "the mask is the outer veil of man, covering not only the face, but the entire body and the whole essence of man. Persona is another word for it. . . . Thus the stage mask is a poetized emanation of the idea of being, an emanation that proclaims this idea in form and color." All of these statements derive, of course, from the declarations of Edward Gordon Craig, who insisted that the mask was "the only right medium of portraying the expressions of the soul." [18]

O'Neill's successful nonrealistic plays, *The Emperor Jones, The Hairy Ape,* and *The Great God Brown,* were effective on the stage primarily because of their portrayal of subjective soul states. These plays possess a dynamism that catapulted American drama into world prominence. For O'Neill enriched native drama with his masterful use of a poetry of aural and visual effects which, as Jean Cocteau pointed out in defining his *poésie de théâtre,* the modern playwright offers as a substitute for verbal poetry in the theatre. O'Neill's skillful projection of his characters' inner states through distorted settings and masks suggests a much closer affinity with the German expressionists than with Strindberg, in whose dream plays the consciousness of not the protagonist but the author holds sway over the surreal action. Unquestionably, O'Neill derived much inspiration from Strindberg, but he also absorbed the basic principles of the contemporary avant-garde theatre of Germany and selected from these the devices that best suited his purposes in dramatic construction. It is with considerable justification, then, that a German critic has referred to him as "the American Georg Kaiser." [19] For Eugene O'Neill was above all a sensitive artist of the theatre. His plays, like those of Kaiser and the expressionists in general, have more power on the stage than in the library.

4

The Provincetown Players
The Triumvirate and After

Jig Cook had already left for Greece when the Province-town Players staged O'Neill's *The Hairy Ape,* their next-to-last production before a hiatus of nearly two years. During this period (1922–23), the group was reorganized under the leadership of Kenneth Macgowan, Robert Edmond Jones, and Eugene O'Neill. When the triumvirate took over, Cook's organization, known as The Provincetown Players, was formally dissolved. It was further agreed that the physical theatre, The Provincetown Playhouse, retain its name, but that the Macgowan-Jones-O'Neill organization call itself The Experimental Theatre, Inc. The public, however, continued to apply the name Provincetown Players to the reorganized theatre.

The new management was firmly committed to experimentation. O'Neill had made a name for himself and the Players as well as for the American drama with his expressionistic *The Emperor Jones* (the first American play to be produced in Paris) and *The Hairy Ape* (which popularized the term *expressionism* in New York). Jones was one of America's leading experimental designers. His abstract settings and masks for Arthur Hopkins's 1921 production of *Macbeth* were hailed as expressionistic by Kenneth Macgowan, who recorded the twilight of realism and heralded an expressionistic "Theatre of Tomorrow" in a book by that name, which appeared also in 1921. In 1922 Macgowan and Jones collaborated on a

book titled *Continental Stagecraft*. Under the management of the triumvirate, the Provincetown Players, who
had previously sustained the experimental talents of Alfred Kreymborg, Susan Glaspell, and the early O'Neill,
entered their expressionist phase.

The expressionistic orientation of the reorganized
Provincetown Players was underscored by O'Neill when
he advised Macgowan about drafting a declaration of
the principles that would govern the new theatre. "I
think you ought to inject a lot of the Kamerny spirit into
your statement," wrote O'Neill to Macgowan in an un-
dated letter (MS in the Yale Library), referring to the
work of the Russian expressionist director Alexander
Tairov at Moscow's Kamerny Theatre. O'Neill also sub-
mitted a list of plays to be staged by the triumvirate:
Walter Hasenclever's *Humanity* (*Die Menschen*, 1920)
or his *Beyond*, "as example of essence of Expressionism
in acting, scenic, everything"; Leonid Andreyev's *The
Black Maskers* or his *King Hunger*; Frank Wedekind's
The Earth Spirit, "done entirely with masks as by a lot
of mannequins"; and August Strindberg's *The Dance of
Death* or *The Ghost Sonata*.

For their first production, on January 3, 1924, the reorganized Provincetown Players gave the American première of *The Ghost Sonata* (which they translated as
The Spook Sonata). It was played with masks at
O'Neill's suggestion. Writing in the playbill, O'Neill
called Strindberg "the precursor of all modernity in our
present theater" and attacked "the banality of surfaces"
by describing theatrical realism as "our Fathers' daring
aspirations toward self-recognition by holding the family
kodak up to ill-nature." [1]

Later in the season (on April 16, 1924), on the same
program with Molière's *George Dandin*, the triumvirate
presented O'Neill's arrangement of Coleridge's *The Ancient Mariner*. O'Neill conceived of the adaption "as a
novel form of recitative, pantomime, Expressionist
drama," [2] in which the action on the stage parallels the
spoken words of the narrator-mariner. As the mariner be-

gins his tale with "There was a ship," six sailors enter
with sections of a stylized ship, assemble it, and go
through the motions of being at sea, acting out in pantomime the story of Coleridge's poem. The unreal quality
of the dramatis personae other than the mariner and the
wedding guest he has detained suggests that the scenes
unfolding on the stage are not to be taken as a realistic
enactment of Coleridge's story, but should be viewed as
subjective projections. Thus the Bride and Groom appear as puppets who dance to Tchaikovsky's "Doll's
Funeral March," two of the wedding guests have "mask-
like faces of smug, complacent dullness" ("they walk
like marionettes," adds O'Neill in the stage directions),
and the six sailors who comprise the chorus appear initially with "the masks of drowned men," which are later
changed to the masks of holy spirits and of angels to de-
note their altered spiritual states.[3] Employing masks then
not only in order to distort reality as seen through the
eyes of the mariner, but also to communicate to the audience the inner states of the characters who wear them
(e.g., the drowned sailors), O'Neill gave to *The Ancient
Mariner* a basically expressionistic handling.

Following a revival of *The Emperor Jones*, the Provincetown Players staged O'Neill's *All God's Chillun Got
Wings* on May 15, 1924. Frequently termed a realistic
study of racial problems, the play is actually deeply expressionistic. It is written in seven relatively short scenes
(divided into two acts); the action is often extremely
stylized and exaggerated (as in the wedding scene); both
Jim, a Negro, and his wife Ella, a white ex-prostitute, become at times type characters representing not so much
their races as human beings caught in their individual
yet universal predicaments; and O'Neill has given the
play a dramatic rhythm based on such sound effects as
the periodic roar of an elevated train, patterned laughter,
and the artificial introduction of songs that express the
mood of the moment. The most effective piece of expressionist dramaturgy in this play is O'Neill's use of distorted settings. As the inner tensions of Jim and Ella

mount, climaxing in Ella's insanely murderous attack on an African mask that adorns their apartment, O'Neill objectifies the suffocation of love in an atmosphere of violent quarrels by having the walls and the ceiling of the apartment gradually move inward.

Though Cleon Throckmorton designed distorted settings for the Provincetown production of *All God's Chillun Got Wings*, O'Neill preferred Tairov's Russian expressionist version of this play. O'Neill saw Tairov's productions of *Desire Under the Elms* and *All God's Chillun Got Wings* in Paris, and in a letter to the Kamerny Theatre, he complimented the Russian director. "Your productions," he wrote, "delighted me because they rang so true to the spirit of my work!" [4] What was there about the Kamerny production of *Chillun* that O'Neill did not find in this country? A possible answer is suggested by an Englishman's account of Tairov's Moscow production of *All God's Chillun Got Wings*. "On the technical side," wrote this observer, "the Moscow production was much better than the London production, especially in the street-scenes, where the devices of Expressionism—though perhaps too assiduously exploited—heightened the tension with the jarring rhythm of New York's traffic noises." That O'Neill clearly intended *Chillun* to be a nonrealistic play is revealed by a comment he made in 1932: "In 'All God's Chillun Got Wings,' all save the seven leading characters should be masked; for all the secondary figures are part and parcel of the Expressionistic background of the play." [5]

The new mode left an imprint also on Edmund Wilson's *The Crime in the Whistler Room*, the next production (October 9, 1924) of the Provincetown Players. As a scholar has quipped, "one of the several crimes in the play is the introduction of expressionistic dream sequences in what is otherwise an ordinary drawing room comedy." [6] *The Crime in the Whistler Room* begins realistically enough in the Long Island country house of a wealthy Boston family. The Streetfields have "rescued" Elizabeth ("Bill") McGee from poverty and ignorance

and are preparing her for college entrance examinations. Bill's current lover is Simon Delacy, a young writer modeled on F. Scott Fitzgerald. Simon's hedonism sets off the stuffiness of the Streetfields and completely overwhelms Bill, who tries throughout the first act to tell him that she is pregnant. The act ends with the beginning of Bill's nightmare, a visual expression of her feelings of entrapment—carrying a bundle in her arms, she runs along a dark corridor, but a guard blocks the doorway.

Act 2 continues the dream sequence, including an objectification of Bill's fears about an impending algebra examination. She is shown "working at an enormous blackboard covered with very large chalked figures," while the tutor sits "on a high stool behind a high desk." [7] Cleon Throckmorton's designs for this scene featured a grotesquely elongated stool and desk, pronounced shadows, a mask for the tutor, and two gigantic blackboards sufficiently askew to suggest the influence of *The Cabinet of Dr. Caligari*. (As was pointed out in the previous chapter, Throckmorton was an admirer of this expressionist film. Wilson, too, speaks highly of *Caligari* in a September 23, 1925, *New Republic* article.)

Bill fails to balance the equation, which has meanwhile assumed an extraalgebraic function—"I can't make Simon's side balance with my side!" (p. 174)—and the nightmare continues with an objectification of Bill's impressions of Simon's new book about the living dead. The corpse in this case is the coupon-clipping Mr. Streetfield, who "is stretched stiff and askew in his chair, as if he had been stricken by paralysis: his lips are parted and show his teeth, and his eyes have a kind of glazed glare" (p. 175). When Bill approaches him, "he suddenly gives a horrible hawking gasp, accompanied by a spasmodic movement of his body," and behaves somewhat like the mummy in Strindberg's *The Ghost Sonata*. The scene ends with the Streetfields "pressing close about [Bill] like fiends" (p. 192). But she refuses to be rescued and made into a college girl.

Act 3 concludes Bill's dream sequence with an idyllic

wish fulfillment of travel and marital happiness that clashes violently with the reality of the next morning— Simon cancels his date with Bill in order to take out another girl. He changes his mind, however, when he learns that she is carrying his child, and the two lovers, shouting their rejection of "both the drudgery of the slaves and the dismal salvation of the masters" depart to "found a race of [their] own" (p. 207). Thus *The Crime in the Whistler Room* not only makes considerable use of expressionistic formal techniques, but projects a message not unlike that of the heralding of the utopian New Man in Georg Kaiser's *The Citizens of Calais* (*Die Bürger von Calais*, 1917) or *Gas I*.

That Wilson knew Continental expressionist literature at first hand is suggested by his references to the new drama in his critical articles of this period, in which he discusses Evreinov's concept of "monodrama" and refers to Kaiser's *From Morn to Midnight*.[8] At the same time Wilson was writing other experimental plays of his own. His tongue in cheek *Fun for Old and Young* (later renamed *The Age of Pericles*), subtitled *An Expressionist Play*, appeared in the *New Republic* for February 24, 1926. Also in 1926 he published *Discordant Encounters: Plays and Dialogues*. The plays in this volume are *The Crime in the Whistler Room* and *Cronkhite's Clocks*. The latter is a grotesque pantomime. The first half of its title derives from the German word *Krankheit*, meaning disease or sickness, and the play satirizes the destructive and dehumanizing effect of mechanization while presenting all the clichés of expressionist distortion. *Cronkhite's Clocks* is reminiscent of the work of the Dadaists, the Triadic Ballet, and Oskar Schlemmer's experiments at the theatre of the Bauhaus. In the *New Republic* for July 30, 1930, Wilson published another short expressionist satire, *Beautiful Old Things*, which records the struggles of a few remaining stone-house people against the pressures of a glass-house civilization.

(Even more hilarious than Wilson's brief satires are the short nonsense plays of Ring Lardner. Among the

most absurd of these are *Cora or Fun at a Spa,* subtitled
An Expressionist Drama of Love and Death and Sex,
and the three playlets published in *What of It?* [1925].
Concerning the latter, Henry Longan Stuart wrote on
the front page of the *New York Times Book Review*
[April 19, 1925], "it seems that the gamut of emotion
aroused and pent up by the Expressionist movement
had waited Mr. Lardner's saving scalpel to find its true
release in uproarious mirth.")

Wilson's *The Crime in the Whistler Room* was the
first production of the 1924–25 Provincetown season.
For the third bill of that season the Players once more
revived *The Emperor Jones.* For the fourth bill (January
26, 1925) they heeded O'Neill's advice and presented
the American première of Walter Hasenclever's *Beyond.*
The production was designed by Robert Edmond Jones,
and Isaac Goldberg, author of *The Drama of Transition*
(1922), grappled with the meaning of the term *expressionism* in the playbill (season 1924–25, no. 4). Goldberg suggested that "Expressionism is an intoxication of
the soul" or "art running a temperature." Hence, at its
best, "it is curiously like those fevers that cleanse the
body and give it a new lease of life." Most critics had
little good to say about *Beyond,* but Stark Young, writing in the *New York Times* (January 27, 1925), urged
everyone interested in modern drama to go to the Provincetown Playhouse and "find out . . . what you think
of the progress of expressionism in drama," for "you will
see at the Provincetown as beautiful arrangements of
scenes and lighting in the expressionistic style as you
will be likely to see anywhere." The Provincetown Playhouse had indeed become a bastion of imported as well
as native expressionism. During the two seasons of its
reign, the triumvirate staged six expressionist plays: *The
Ghost* (or as they called it, *The Spook*) *Sonata, The
Ancient Mariner, All God's Chillun Got Wings, The
Crime in the Whistler Room, Beyond,* and a revival of
The Emperor Jones.

Expressionism continued to give a particular coloring

to the work of the Provincetown Players even after Macgowan, Jones, and O'Neill left the group to establish an independent producing unit in the Greenwich Village Theater (where they staged O'Neill's *The Great God Brown*). The first production of the Provincetown Players under the direction of James Light and M. Eleanor Fitzgerald was Em Jo Basshe's *Adam Solitaire* (November 6, 1925). I have not been able to locate a copy of the manuscript of this unpublished play, but the reviews place it firmly in the expressionist tradition.

According to the *New York Times* (November 7, 1925), Basshe's *Adam Solitaire* began "in the usual objective manner of the theatre," but then became "increasingly expressionistic, and increasingly incoherent withal," while depicting "the transmogrification of a young man's soul, against a background of triangular, unbalanced buildings, and to the chant of fiends and demoniacs." The *Herald Tribune* reviewer (November 7, 1925) assumed that Basshe had been an ardent student of such expressionists as Georg Kaiser and praised Cleon Throckmorton's "admirable and imaginative" settings that "trace directly to those magnificently distorted scenes from the . . . 'Cabinet of Dr. Caligari.' " In *The Drama* (January 1926), Barrett H. Clark, who had published articles on German expressionist playwrights, some of whom he had met in Europe, declared that he knew "something about the young Germans who served . . . Basshe as models." Photographs of the production support this view. How closely the Provincetown Players had been linked with expressionism by the time they produced Basshe's play is suggested by the comments of the *New York Times* reviewer, who wonders in his Sunday column (November 15, 1925) why the Provincetown Players selected *Adam Solitaire* as the first production of their new season and then answers his own question, "One suspects that the play was chosen for its technique—expressionism."

A touch of expressionist staging in the last act livened the otherwise realistic production of Charles Webster's

The Man Who Never Died, which the Players gave as their second bill of the 1925–26 season (December 12, 1925), and for the third bill of the season they staged the American première of Strindberg's *A Dream Play* (January 20, 1926). The next season of the Province-town Players began on November 12, 1926, with an example of Russian expressionism when Leo Bulgakov of the Moscow Art Theatre directed Carlo Gozzi's *Princess Turandot* in the manner of Eugene Vakhtan-gov's celebrated 1922 version of that play.

Turandot was followed on December 30, 1926, by Paul Green's *In Abraham's Bosom.* The tragic story of a mulatto who tries to educate Southern Negroes, the Pulitzer Prize-winning *In Abraham's Bosom* grew out of Green's earlier one-act plays. Both *Your Fiery Furnace,* a 1923 revision of *Sam Tucker,* and the 1924 short ver-sion of *In Abraham's Bosom,* which went into the mak-ing of the full-length play, are realistic. One of the new scenes, however, externalizes the protagonist's inner tur-moil. Having killed his white half-brother, Abraham McCranie experiences the horror of his deed as "the branches of the trees seem to change their characteristics and become a wild seething of mocking, menacing hands stretched forth from all sides at him." [9] This is clearly reminiscent of the well-known episode in Kaiser's *From Morn to Midnight* (produced in 1922 by the Theatre Guild), in which a tree turns into a skeleton, thus objectifying the suicidal thoughts of the Cashier. As in *From Morn to Midnight*—and O'Neill's *The Emperor Jones*—Green then presents the protagonist's visions of the events that have profoundly affected his life. In pantomimic action we see the lynching that incited Abraham to struggle for Negroes' rights. An-other dumb show depicts his mother going into the bushes with a white man in an act of miscegenation. In a letter to the present writer (August 21, 1967), Green suggests several sources, among them the plays of Ger-man expressionism, that motivated him in creating this scene of subjective distortion. "I am sure," writes Green, "that my reading in German expressionistic drama, seeing [Stuart] Walker's dreamy production of 'The Book of Job,' and swallowing joyously and wholeheartedly 'Emperor Jones' made it easier for me to create such a scene."

Following *In Abraham's Bosom*, the Provincetown Players produced Lajos N. Egri's *Rapid Transit* on April 7, 1927. Egri has published several books on how to write, which disclose a mind apparently unsullied by thoughts of formal experimentation. Yet in *Rapid Transit* he reveals his indebtedness to expressionist dramaturgy. The play opens with a visually effective scene—a great wheel snatches a man from a prison cell and deposits him in the chamber of a complicated mechanism with "innumerable interlocking wheels which wind and rewind each other." [10] "Where am I?" asks the dazed protagonist, Imre Szabo. There is no answer. Instead, "softly and silently the wheels keep on turning" (p. 1–1). Eventually a voice speaks "in a mechanical way in keeping with the tempo of the winding wheels" (p. 1–2) and supplies the necessary answers. *Rapid Transit* records Szabo's adventure in this strange new world where people worship the Great Wheel and pay a breathing and walking tax, and where a lifetime is compressed into twenty-four hours.

The play is in six scenes and a prologue; parts of it, writes Egri in a "Note for the Producer," should be played "in somewhat of a staccato manner" and "the exterior scenes be put out of focus from the point of view of the audience;" most of the characters are types; and the language is frequently abbreviated. For *Rapid Transit* is an objectification of the rapid pace of life in a machine-dominated materialistic country. The scene involving stock transactions is reminiscent of the episode with the fox-trotting bankers in Ernst Toller's *Man and the Masses* (which the Theatre Guild produced in 1924); the Six Gossips behave like the Mmes. One through Six in Elmer Rice's *The Adding Machine* (1923); and as in O'Neill's *All God's Chillun Got Wings*, the walls of a room move inward when Szabo is tormented by the suspicion that his wife may have been unfaithful to him.

As the *New York Herald Tribune* reviewer of *Rapid Transit* pointed out (April 8, 1927), "If Ernst Toller had never been heard of. . . . if, in short, the expressionistic 'Rapid Transit' . . . had come over the horizon several years ago, there's no telling how remarkable it might have seemed." As it was, Egri's play appeared to be highly derivative. The *Times* critic (April 8, 1927) rendered a basically similar verdict, establishing in the process once more the claim of the Provincetown theatre to the name of "Macdougal Street's foremost expressionistic playhouse." Other reviewers noted the resemblance of *Rapid Transit* to Fritz Lang's *Metropolis*, a German expressionist film depicting mechanized mankind and released in the United States in 1927.

Rapid Transit closed the Provincetown's 1926–27 season. For the final bill of their 1927–28 season, on April 18, 1928, the Players gave E. E. Cummings's *Him*. Like T. S. Eliot's "The Love Song of J. Alfred Prufrock," *Him* begins with "a patient etherized upon a table"—a doctor is anesthetizing a woman. Her eyes close and the play unfolds as an objectification of her thoughts and memories, with the doctor reappearing in different roles throughout the play. Unlike the sterile Prufrock, however, the woman in *Him* is about to give birth to a child, and the play is a subjectively distorted presentation of her affair with the father of the child. He is a playwright who grapples with the problem of art and reality. Creating an image similar to the one used by Jean Cocteau in the preface to his play *Orphée* (1926), in which the French playwright describes art in terms of balancing on a tightrope without a safety net, Him, the protagonist of the woman's dream, speaks of "circustent[s]" and "slackwire tightrope[s]" and defines the artist as "a human being who balances three chairs, one on top of another, on a wire, eighty feet in air with no net underneath, and then climbs into the top chair, sits down, and begins to swing." [11]

The three chairs, says Him, are three facts: "I am an

Artist, I am a Man, I am a Failure" (p. 11). Seen through the ether dream of Me, the woman, Him's dilemma involves his inability to fuse beauty (art) and truth (love). As the expressionistically objectified drumbeats of Me's labor pains heighten in act 3, scene 5, Me (who has sacrificed her happiness with Him for Him's art and has left Him) remembers a conversation in which Him admits that "beauty [i.e., art] has shut me from truth [i.e., love]" (p. 100). The play ends with Him still unable to accept "truth." However, by the time Cummings delivered the 1953 Charles Eliot Norton Lectures at Harvard, the artist in him had evidently mastered the balancing act of life by reconciling beauty and truth, art and love. "Art is a mystery," said Cummings at that time. "All mysteries have their source in a mystery-of-mysteries who is love: and if lovers may reach eternity directly through love herself, their mystery remains essentially that of the loving artist whose way must lie through his art." [12]

In *Him*, Cummings's concern with the ego of the artist, with the *Ausstrahlungen* of his own *Ichs*, as the Germans would put it, is characteristically expressionistic. In form, too, Cummings rebelled against the conventions of realistic dramaturgy. Reviewing a performance of the visiting Moscow Art Theatre Musical Studio in the April 1926 issue of the *Dial*, Cummings spoke derisively of the "pennyintheslot peepshow parlour" proscenium stage, for which should be substituted "an aesthetic continent," where tourists pay their way in "constructivist" or "expressionist" currency.

Part of the expressionist currency in *Him* involves the chorus of the three Miss Weirds—or Fates—who wear identical maskfaces and, like the ladies in Alfred Kreymborg's *Rocking Chairs* (published in 1925), speak in non sequiturs and rock in chairs. The scenes between Him and Me contain spoken thoughts and surreal language full of distorted dream images. For example, when Me sees Him with a (phallic) pistol in his hand, Him hastily explains, "Pistil. The female organ of a flower. . . . in three parts, ovary style and stigma" (p. 19). The episode with the pistol, which Him aims at his head while staring at his "other self" in the mirror, introduces the visual handling of the concept of multiple personalities.

As in O'Neill's *The Great God Brown*, in which Margaret loves the mask of her husband, in Cummings's play, Him thinks Me loves the Other Man in him. Whereas O'Neill used masks to differentiate between conflicting selves, Cummings uses a similarly visual device, a hat. In act 1, scene 4, Him tells Me that his hat is really the Other Man's hat and that it is the Other Man who is Me's lover. To prove it, Him leads Me to the mirror, where he points to Mr. Mirror Man, which Me identifies as "O. Him" (p. 22), thus setting up a relationship between the protagonist and his alter ego that brings to mind *The Great God Brown* as well as Franz Werfel's *Mirror-Man*. In act 3, scene 5, Him's hat has disappeared, and Him tells Me how he killed a man with a crumpled hat. The dialogue at this point creates an atmosphere of paradox that brings to mind the complex relationship between the conflicting selves of the protagonist in the O'Neill play.

HIM   . . . I didn't talk to him [the other man].
ME   Why?
HIM   Because I killed him.
ME   [*Starting violently*].—The man?
HIM   Himself.
ME   —You didn't—
HIM   Kill him?
ME   —him—
HIM   O, him. [*Easily*] Of course I didn't. [*Smiles*]— Just the other way 'round.
ME   [*Earnestly*]. What do you mean?
HIM   It's clear now—can't you see? [*Gently*] He killed me. (P. 93)

In 1926, when O'Neill's *The Great God Brown* was produced, Cummings reported on the New York theatre scene in the *Dial*, and in act 2, scene 4, of *Him* he parodies O'Neill's use of masks and the complicated business of Billy Brown's murder. In Cummings's play, Bill and Will are seen in an office. Will's maskface resembles the real face of the Intruder. Will goes to shoot the Intruder, but instead kills himself, whereupon the Intruder assumes Will's seat. The dead man's real face is then revealed to correspond to Bill's maskface. The Intruder accuses Bill of killing Will for a woman.

The nine scenes of act 2 of *Him* (corresponding, like the nine freaks in act 3, scene 6, and the appearance of the doctor in nine different roles, to the nine months of Me's pregnancy) are scenes from Him's—or possibly The Other Man's—play. Recollected by Me in her ether dream, these scenes contain considerable distortion and objectification, as in the case of the formally dressed Englishman who staggers under a huge trunk that holds his unconscious (scene 6). Cummings's language often resembles that of Yvan Goll, and as Eric Bentley has pointed out in his analysis of *Him*, act 2, scene 9, is "noticeably influenced" by European expressionism.[13] That Cummings was familiar with expressionist drama is further suggested by his references to native experimentalists, including Kreymborg and O'Neill, in a 1925 *Vanity Fair* parody, "Seven Samples of Dramatic Criticism."

Most reviewers of *Him* either did not understand the play or made no effort to do so. Yet theatregoers kept flocking to the Provincetown Playhouse. The Players were exhilarated and published a pamphlet titled *him AND the CRITICS*. Included among the appreciative comments in the pamphlet were Edmund Wilson's statement that "our American expressionist dramas have too often been deficient in precisely those elements in which Cummings' is rich" and a note by S. Foster Damon, who classified *Him* in the tradition of Strindberg, Dada, and O'Neill. Cummings's use of "all the Expressionists' rattling stage properties" has been noted, furthermore, by Jaques Barzun, who witnessed the origi-

nal Provincetown production; and commenting on ex-
pressionistic symbols in his *Theory and Technique of
Playwriting,* John Howard Lawson offers as examples
Hasenclever's *Beyond* and Cummings's *Him.*[14]

For their 1928–29 season, the Players revived Paul
Green's *In Abraham's Bosom* and then staged *The Final Balance* by the Yiddish playwright David Pinski
(October 30, 1928). Pinski's melodramatic work (ms
in the Library of Congress) focuses on a greedy flour
merchant and contains a grotesque street scene (act 4,
scene 1) with characters who have become insane. Mordecai Gorelik's distorted settings reminded reviewers of
The Cabinet of Dr. Caligari and effectively reflected the
expressionistic tone of the scene.

For the next bill, the Provincetowners turned the
playhouse over to the New Playwrights for their production of Upton Sinclair's expressionistic *Singing Jailbirds,* which will be discussed in Chapter Seven. (Earlier
in 1928 the Players had offered their theatre to The
Actor-Managers, Inc., whose production of French expressionist playwright Simon Gantillon's *Maya* had been
closed by the district attorney's office. Because of police
pressure, the Actor-Managers declined the offer.) On
November 18, in the hopes of raising funds for a commercial production of O'Neill's *Lazarus Laughed*
(which never materialized), the Players gave a reading
of that play for an invited audience of potential con-
tributors.

Lazarus Laughed, like *The Great God Brown,* is a
play of masks, and the entire work may very well be an
attempt on the part of O'Neill to objectify the moment
of Lazarus' death. Though most commentators on the
play have found fault with it, Lothar Schreyer, one of
the original German expressionists, considers *Lazarus
Laughed* to be the ultimate in expressionist drama:
"The work is so significant as poetry and inner vision of
the theatre—of imaginative theatre—that it towers above
the fleeting quality of all the German expressionist
'word-productions' [*Wortkunstwerke*] for the stage. It

can be said to continue creatively on the road of the theatre as defined by the understanding acquired from expressionism." [15]

In the fall of 1929 the Provincetown Players made plans to produce Paul Green's *Tread the Green Grass*. Subtitled *A Folk Fantasy in Two Parts With Interludes, Music, Dumb-show, and Cinema,* Green's expressionist play ("to be produced with masks when possible") tells the story of Tina, a southern farm girl who, like O'Neill's Dion Anthony, is torn between pagan acceptance of life and Christian rejection of worldly pleasures. In the first scene Tina falls asleep and her dream materializes on the stage—"out of the gloom of her dream . . . come creeping an Old Man and an Old Woman." They are grotesquely dressed, move in the manner of "furtive animals," and wear masks.[16] The eerie couple motion for Tina to follow them. In the next scene, a dream vision, she visits the forest lair of the mysterious couple. There she meets Young Davie. In creating this character, Green (whose *In Aunt Mahaly's Cabin*, written in 1924, bears a certain resemblance to O'Neill's *The Emperor Jones*) may have been influenced by *The Great God Brown,* for Young Davie capers like Pan and appears to Tina with a "malicious and devilish mask which looks saintlike to her" (p. 240), thus suggesting several parallels with O'Neill's Dion Anthony. When queried on this point, Green wrote the present writer (August 21, 1967) that though he did not care much for the "mushy and sentimental" dialogue in *The Great God Brown,* he "did admire the use of masks insofar as they helped along the breaking of the bonds of American theatre production."

In the next scene of *Tread the Green Grass,* Tina participates in a nightmarish supper with her parents and five preachers. Three of the preachers are dressed exactly alike and speak in unison. Then follow a panoramic interlude, with the action involving the entire countryside, and a long pantomimic scene in a church, where the congregation is divided into two groups, the middle-aged men and women sitting on one side of the center aisle and the young people on the other. Penitents, eager to testify, rise up "like jacks-in-the-box" (p. 283), and a young girl "babbles" (p. 284) her thanks to the Lord. When Tina falls senseless to the floor, Green symbolizes the impotence of formal religion by the failure of the preachers to bring her back to life. Young Davie, on the other hand, representing Eros against the preachers' Thanatos, succeeds in resurrecting her, whereupon the young people engage in a Dionysiac orgy that brings to mind Franz Werfel's *Goat Song,* which the Theatre Guild presented in January of 1926.

In the Werfel play, act 4 of which takes place in a village church, "the women shake out their unbound hair and begin to tear their clothes." [17] In *Tread the Green Grass,* "the young girls throw off their hats, undo their hair—they open the bosoms of their dresses and beautify themselves. The young men pursue them round and round, catch them and caress them" (p. 290). Following another cinematic interlude, Tina, like the bride in *Goat Song* who gives herself to the monster, worships Young Davie, who suddenly appears as "a figure with goatish beard, thick sausage lips, hairy like a dog" (p. 300), thus suggesting yet another parallel with the Werfel play. At the end of *Tread the Green Grass,* Tina goes insane, and we realize that the entire play has been an objectification of the protagonist's inner state. When asked about the indebtedness of his play to *Goat Song,* Green told the present writer, "I remember . . . that I read it back in 1926, and it may have influenced me."

Green's experimental dramaturgy has been attributed to the influence of the Moscow State Jewish Theatre, whose expressionistic productions he saw in Berlin in 1928–29.[18] However, *Tread the Green Grass* was written in 1927–28. So were several of his other plays that contain touches of expressionistic objectification and distortion, such as *Supper for the Dead* and *The Man on the House,* which later became *Shroud My Body Down.* As a playwright interested in the theatre of his day,

Green was undoubtedly acquainted with the plays of
German as well as native expressionism before he went
to Germany in 1928, for in the case of *Tread the Green
Grass*, there is a strong affinity not only with Euripides'
The Bacchae, but specifically with Werfel's *Goat Song*
and O'Neill's *The Great God Brown*.

Yet at that time Green would probably not have
agreed to being labeled an expressionist. In his preface
to the fourth series of *One-Act Plays for Stage and
Study*, published in 1928, he describes a visit to an art
theatre. He comments on what seems to be the set for
the Provincetown production of Lajos Egri's *Rapid
Transit* ("a man is caught upon [the Wheel of Time]
and in its turning Time is changed, and a whole life
unrolls before us in the space of two hours") and notes
that "lacking the power of words we've taken refuge in
mechanics." In this preface Green states, furthermore,
that he does not believe in the theatre of Gordon Craig,
and he likens theatrical masks that represent different
selves to gasmasks. Now, however, when reminded of
his own use of masks in such plays as *Tread the Green
Grass* and *Shroud My Body Down*, Green is less eager
to disassociate himself from the expressionists. "My
visualizing masks in these plays," he informed the
present writer, "showed that I had repented or forgot
my first denial of them in relation to Gordon Craig."
Green's subsequent development as a playwright, before he turned to composing historical outdoor page-
ants, bears out his revised views on Craig and the expressionists.

In 1928 Green went to Germany, "because he felt the
theatre there was venturing into experimental fields."
In Berlin he saw plays of subjective expressionism and
was impressed by the work of the visiting Moscow State
Jewish Theatre. From Berlin he went to England, where
parts of Sean O'Casey's *The Silver Tassie* "got hold" of
him.[19] Elements of the expressionistic second act of *The
Silver Tassie* thus found their way into act 2, scene 3, of
Green's *Johnny Johnson* (1936), an antiwar musical on
which he collaborated with Kurt Weill.

Though the Provincetown Players rehearsed *Tread the Green Grass*, the production was canceled about a week before opening night. (Green's play was eventually given at the University of Iowa on July 15, 1932.) The Provincetown board apparently dropped the production of *Tread the Green Grass* because they needed a potential commercial success. Yet neither the substitution of Louis Bromfield's *Fun* nor the generous pledges of support by wealthy patrons were able to save the theatre when the stock market crashed in October of 1929. A decade, a way of life, and a great experimental theatre expired in that crash.

Perhaps the Provincetown Players' most important contribution to American drama was their encouragement, originally proclaimed by Jig Cook, of native playwrights. As the triumvirate assumed control, the Players became dedicated also to experimentation. The plays of Alfred Kreymborg, Eugene O'Neill, Susan Glaspell, Edmund Wilson, E. E. Cummings, and Paul Green would no doubt have been written anyway. Nevertheless, the Provincetown Playhouse provided native playwrights with a laboratory in which to experiment with new dramatic forms. The Provincetown was not, however, the only proving ground for new dramaturgical ideas in the 1920s. Experimental playwrights such as Elmer Rice and John Howard Lawson found hospitable accommodations under the roof of the Theatre Guild.

5

Elmer Rice

Two months after Eugene O'Neill's *The Hairy Ape* opened at the Provincetown Playhouse in the early spring of 1922, the Theatre Guild produced Georg Kaiser's *From Morn to Midnight*. The production, originally scheduled for four subscription performances, caught public attention and soon moved into a larger theatre for an extended run. To the rapid pacing of scenes, Lee Simonson's imaginative sets, and the utilization of strongly lighted areas surrounded by darkness, the Guild added the use of the Linnebach projector in order to create the transformation of a tree and a chandelier into a skeleton and to objectify the death wish of the protagonist. New York theatregoers, who had been stirred by *The Hairy Ape*, were at long last able to see a genuine German expressionist play.

The Theatre Guild had grown out of the Washington Square Players, which boasted an impressive record of productions of European avant-garde drama. In addition to plays by Maeterlinck, Strindberg, and Wedekind, the Players had given Nikolai Evreinov's *A Merry Death* (1916) as well as Leonid Andreyev's *Love of One's Neighbor* (1915) and *The Life of Man* (1917). Among the native plays staged at the Bandbox Theatre had been an anonymous Evreinovesque divertissement entitled *Another Interior* (1915), the action of which took place inside a stomach during dinner. The cast included such delicacies as An Oyster, Three Sauces, and An Irresistible Liqueur. Of the numerous Guild productions of foreign plays (in addition to *From Morn to Midnight*), mention should be made of Andreyev's *He Who Gets Slapped* (1922), Karel Čapek's *R.U.R.* (1922), Theodore Kommisarjevsky's expressionist staging of Ibsen's *Peer Gynt* (1923), Henri-René Lenormand's *Failures* (1923), Ernst Toller's *Man and the Masses* (1924), Franz Werfel's *Goat Song* (1926), and Evreinov's *The Chief Thing* (1926). As Lawrence Langner, one of the founders of the Guild, has pointed out in his memoirs, "it was my feeling, as well as that of the rest of the Guild board, that we should produce the important plays of European authors to set a standard for American writers." [1] When native dramatists achieved recognition, the Guild did encourage them by staging their plays. O'Neill, for example, began his association with this group in 1928.

Of the six O'Neill plays produced by the Guild between 1928 and 1934, three are marked by obvious expressionistic distortions. In *Marco Millions* (January 9, 1928) the countries through which Marco travels resemble one another because the audience sees them with the materialistic eyes of the protagonist. *Dynamo* (February 11, 1929) continues the device of spoken thoughts with which O'Neill experimented in *Welded* (1924) and which made his *Strange Interlude* the talk of the town in 1928. The rather ordered spoken thoughts of O'Neill's characters lack, however, the true stream-of-consciousness approach of a James Joyce and hence fail to objectify the chaotic state of a person's mind. Thus it is rather the visual aspect of *Dynamo* that is relevant here. For the setting of the play calls for a certain amount of subjective distortion, as when Reuben admires the dynamo, which appears to have "a gross, rounded torso." [2] As Reuben's obsession with the "Dynamo-Mother" approaches lunacy, O'Neill again describes the equipment in the power plant in terms of human anatomy, thus revealing Reuben's confusion about his sexual passion for Ada and his mother-worshiping of electricity. The grotesque industrial setting of *Dynamo* as well as its underlying idea of the victory of machines over man brings to mind Georg Kaiser's *Gas*, which had been staged in Chicago in 1926.

O'Neill's *Days Without End* (January 8, 1934) objectifies the dual personality of its protagonist. The two sides of John Loving—John, the believer, and Loving, the atheist—appear simultaneously on the stage: "LOV-ING's face is a mask whose features reproduce exactly the features of JOHN's face—the death mask of a JOHN who has died with a sneer of scornful mockery on his lips" (III, 493–94). Commentators on O'Neill have pointed out certain parallels between this play and Strindberg's *To Damascus* trilogy as well as Werfel's *Mirror-Man*, in which Thamal struggles with his evil mirror image. At the conclusion of Werfel's play, Thamal's alter ego returns into the mirror. As the struggle between the two sides of John Loving's personality resolves itself, the atheistic Loving "slumps forward to the floor and rolls over on his back, dead," while John, standing before a large figure of Christ crucified, extends his arms up and out like a cross, thus repeating the final image of Kaiser's *From Morn to Midnight*.

From Morn to Midnight may also have influenced Elmer Rice, one of the first American playwrights to have his work produced by the Theatre Guild. Born as Elmer Leopold Reizenstein into a German-American family, Rice was trained as a lawyer. His first love, however, was the theatre. "By 1909," he once remarked, "I was a confirmed theatregoer. I went to the Irving Place Theatre to see plays in German." [3] His first commercially successful play, *On Trial*, which made effective use of the then novel device of the flashback, dates from 1914. But it was not until March 18, 1923, when the Theatre Guild produced his *The Adding Machine*, that he unveiled his most durable play. In this work Rice depicts the mind and soul of Mr. Zero, a department store bookkeeper, by means of visual distortions.

Like O'Neill, Rice has denied having read the German expressionists.[4] Nevertheless, most reviewers of the Theatre Guild production of *The Adding Machine* recognized his debt to the new form. For example, the *New York Times* critic (March 20, 1923) called Rice's play "the best and fairest example of the newer expressionism in the theatre that [New York] has yet experienced," noting a few days later in his weekly summary of recent openings that "the foreign influence in it was evident to those who had witnessed the efforts of the newer German storm-and-stress men." Rice, however, complained in a letter to the *Times* (April 1, 1923) that reviewers had indiscriminately compared his play to a number of recently produced experimental works, including Wedekind's *Spring's Awakening*, O'Neill's *The Hairy Ape*, and Kaiser's *From Morn to Midnight*. Yet he agreed that all of these plays "attempt to go beyond mere representation and to arrive at interpretation." He then proceeded to define "interpretation" in terms of expressionism: "The author attempts not so much to depict events faithfully as to convey to the spectator what seems to him their inner significance. To achieve this end the dramatist often finds it expedient to depart entirely from objective reality and to employ symbols, condensations and a dozen devices which, to the conservative, must seem arbitrarily fantastic. This, I suppose, is what is meant by expressionism."

In a memorandum to Dudley Digges, who played Mr. Zero in the Theatre Guild production, Rice characterized the protagonist of *The Adding Machine* as "a man who is at once an individual and a type" and pointed out that "in the expressionistic play we subordinate and even discard objective reality and seek to express the character in terms of his own inner life." [5] Furthermore, Rice has defined the process of creation as an impulse on the part of the artist to "get his trouble off his mind or off his chest . . . by symbolically externalizing it." In stating that "thus, literally, [the artist] presses it out, or expresses it," [6] Rice's diction echoes James Joyce's statement of the aesthetics of expressionism in *A Por-*

trait of the Artist as a Young Man: "To speak of [aesthetic matters] and to try to understand their nature and, having understood it, to try slowly and humbly and constantly *to express, to press out again,* from the gross earth or what it brings forth, from sound and shape and colour which are the prison gates of our soul, an image of the beauty we have come to understand—that is art."[7] Like some of the Continental expressionists, Joyce may have been influenced by Benedetto Croce's *Estetica;* the Irish novelist's preoccupation with epiphanies and the concept of *quidditas,* a Thomistic term signifying the "whatness" or "soul" of a thing, reminds one of the expressionists' search for the essence.

Rice's pursuit of essences is revealed most forcefully in *The Adding Machine,* which opens in a cagelike room, lighted by a single naked bulb. "The walls are papered with sheets of foolscap covered with columns of figures,"[8] suggesting the machine-dominated state of mind of the slight and partially bald protagonist, who lies silently on a bed. Thus before a single word is spoken, Rice has conveyed to the audience the substance of his theme by means of expressionistically distorted visual imagery.

The entire first scene consists of Mrs. Zero's long soliloquy, preparing the audience for her husband's drab life in an office, revealed in the next scene. Here Mr. Zero and his coworker Miss Daisy Diana Dorothea Devore—not too distant relatives of the Cashier in Kaiser's *From Morn to Midnight*—sit on high stools in front of tall desks, suggestive of the insignificance of the common man in the modern world and reminiscent of the scene with officials on high chairs in *The Cabinet of Dr. Caligari.* Zero and Daisy, two ciphers cowed by the machine age, enter figures upon a large sheet of paper and engage in stylized thought-dialogue.

When the Boss tells Zero that an adding machine will take his place, Rice objectifies the turmoil in the little man's head. Merry-go-round music is heard, and the floor of the office begins to revolve. As the awareness of the fact that he has been fired sinks deeper into Zero's consciousness, "the music becomes gradually louder and the revolutions more rapid." Rice distorts even the language of the Boss's apology, reducing it only to those words that penetrate into the dazed brain of Mr. Zero: "I'm sorry—no other alternative—greatly regret—old employee—efficiency—economy—business—*business*—BUSINESS—." The fired bookkeeper had expected a raise. The shock of the unexpected news unbalances his mind. Zero murders the Boss. The audience does not see this act of violence, however, for Rice merely presents through aural and visual means Zero's subjective impulse to commit murder:

> *The platform is revolving rapidly now.* ZERO *and the* Boss *face each other. They are entirely motionless save for the* Boss's *jaws, which open and close incessantly. But the words are inaudible. The music swells and swells. To it is added every offstage effect of the theatre. . . . Suddenly it culminates in a terrific peal of thunder. For an instant there is a flash of red and then everything is plunged into blackness.* [Pp. 29–30]

Lee Simonson's setting for the Guild production included not only a revolving turntable and the appropriate sound effects, but also the projection of red blotches and whirling numbers on a screen, thus expressing in visual terms the essence of the filing clerk's aroused yet basically mechanistic mind.

In the following scene the audience views an evening at the home of the Zeros through the protagonist's eyes. The walls of the room are once more covered with sheets of digit-laden foolscap; Mrs. Zero talks incessantly; the doorbell rings with "a sharp clicking such as is made by the operation of the keys and levers of an adding machine" (p. 35); the robotlike guests, known simply as Mr. and Mrs. One, Mr. and Mrs. Two, and so forth, are as machine-stamped as Zero—they enter in a double column; they are dressed alike, reminiscent in their vacuous uniformity of the Fifth Avenue crowd in O'Neill's *The Hairy Ape*; their disconnected, banal, cliché-ridden conversation, occasionally chanted in unison, is given in a staccato rhythm.

Zero's trial takes place in a cell-like courtroom. Again, through distorted visual means, Rice conveys to the audience the protagonist's (and perhaps his own) views on the administration of justice. The jury, composed of Messrs. One, Two, Three, Four, Five, Six, and their wives, sits rigidly. In the Guild production, the judge (who does not appear in the printed text) wore a stony mask. In his soliloquy before the jurors, Zero reveals his inability to escape from the world of mechanization, for he (like the protagonist of Alfred Kreymborg's *Jack's House*) is unable to stop talking about numbers. The scene ends with the jurors shouting in unison "*GUILTY!*"

The Guild production underscored Zero's bewilderment by using distorted scenery. As reported by Ludwig Lewisohn in the *Nation* (April 4, 1923), "The tall windows [of the palace of justice] are crooked; the railing is crooked. But the lines are not crinkled. To the perverse vision they may seem straight. They lean diagonally." Once more, shades of *Dr. Caligari*! As in the case of O'Neill's *The Hairy Ape*, the German film acted as a catalyst in shaping Rice's dramaturgy in *The Adding Machine*. For in a letter to the present writer (May 7, 1964) Rice said that he saw *The Cabinet of Dr. Caligari* "at a private screening in the old Goldwyn studio, in Culver City [California], in 1919 or 1920." "Most of my colleagues scoffed at it," added Rice, "but I was greatly impressed by the film (as I have been upon subsequent viewings). I certainly did not have the film in mind when I wrote The Adding Machine, though what its unconscious influence may have been, it is, of course, impossible for me to know."

In scene 5, which was omitted when the play was originally produced, Zero is imprisoned in a large cage. His prisoner's uniform has very broad stripes, and he eats from an enormous plate with a large wooden spoon,[9] thus magnifying in characteristically expressionistic manner his preoccupation with such prosaic concerns as food on the eve of his execution, for his last request consists of eight courses of ham and eggs.

The conversing corpses in the next scene, which takes place in a graveyard, are somewhat reminiscent of the characters in the last scene of Wedekind's *Spring's Awakening*. The description of Zero's new job, for which he is readied in a celestial "repair and service station," reminds one of the scene in Kaiser's *Gas I* in which the German playwright pictures the monotonous movements of a worker's foot in controlling a block-switch. For Zero's sole responsibility in operating a "super-hyper-adding machine" consists of releasing a lever with the great toe of his right foot. Like Kaiser, Rice castigates modern industrial procedures that atrophy man's soul by demanding from him only the mechanical use of his limbs.

The scene opens with an expressionistic setting rivaled only by that of the murder in scene 2. Zero, wearing a full-dress suit and working at a celestial adding machine, is trapped by the billows of white paper that flow from the machine. The mechanical precision with which he presses the keys and pulls the lever objectifies the working of a mind turned into a machine. For the Guild production, Lee Simonson designed a huge adding machine that dominated the stage, and Rice's stage directions call for the tape to assume menacing proportions —"it covers the floor and the furniture, it climbs the walls and chokes the doorways" (p. 123). Zero thus symbolizes man in an ever-increasing mechanical society, void of identity and enslaved by the monster he has created.

The modest success of *The Adding Machine* may have influenced its author to attempt another expressionist play. Yet Rice experienced great difficulty in placing the script of *The Subway* (which he wrote in 1923) with commercial producers. By the time he returned from Europe in 1928, having there met Henri-René Lenormand and Walter Hasenclever,[10] *The Subway* was in the hands of the Lenox Hill Players, who occupied the Cherry Lane Theatre in Greenwich Village. The production opened on January 25, 1929.

Though Rice has said that *The Subway*, like *The Adding Machine*, deals with "the slavery of the machine-age," [11] an analysis of the expressionistic techniques that comprise the most vivid aural and visual moments of the play suggests that the work owes as much to erotic considerations as to economic impulses. For in *The Subway* Rice objectifies the sexual fears and fantasies of a young woman named Sophie Smith. Thus when a man stares at her in scene 1, Sophie literally feels naked; "her dress becomes diaphanous, revealing the outlines of her figure." [12] Scene 2 finds Sophie in the subway during the rush hour. A crowd of seemingly beastly men surround her, and Rice externalizes Sophie's repulsion at feeling their bodies press against her by means of a simple but theatrically effective expressionist technique. As the flickering lights of the subway black out, the men don "hideous, grotesque, animal masks" (p. 31).

As in *The Adding Machine*, grotesque visual images establish the mood of the next scene, which takes place in Sophie's home. "The broad, vertical stripes of the wall-paper," writes Rice, "suggest the bars of a cage" (p. 35). The members of her family pay no attention to her; their actions are "mechanized and rhythmic" (p. 36); and they objectify their thoughts by speaking them. Her father and brother mechanically read newspaper headlines; her mother thinks audibly about the wisdom of having children; and her sister, again vocalizing her thoughts, fumes at having been deserted by her husband, thus foreshadowing Sophie's own fate. The restraining atmosphere of her home life is heightened toward the end of the scene by the lowering of a curtain of broad vertical strips between Sophie and the audience. The visual image of a tiny cell-like room is used once more in scene 4 and is developed by means of an anxiety dream in Sophie's somewhat disconnected soliloquy that comprises the entire episode.

Scene 5 takes place in the balcony of a motion picture theatre. Here Rice objectifies Eugene's seduction of Sophie by having it parallel the action on the screen. By reading aloud the subtitles of a mythical silent film, Sophie in fact comments on what is actually happening to her. For example, as Eugene presses her hand, she thinks audibly, "Oh, he's hurting me—he's hurting me! He'll break my fingers." In counterpoint to her spoken thoughts, Sophie then reads an appropriately melodramatic subtitle, " 'You're a beast, Lord Orville—a vile beast,' " which is followed by more audible thinking: "I can feel his nails. They're digging into me. Go on! Hurt me some more" (p. 78). In the next scene, before consummating their illicit love, Eugene briefly struggles with his conscience, represented by a toneless, impersonal voice that calls him a liar.

Deflowered and about to be deserted by her lover, Sophie has an inevitable expressionistic nightmare in scene 8. Accusing fingers shoot out at her from the blackness surrounding her bed, and she hears a number of voices. They tell her that she has been fired from her job for committing adultery, that her parents have turned her out of their home, that she has been sentenced for a term in a reformatory, that she will die while undergoing an abortion, and that her child will be a bastard. The longest sustained speech in this scene is spoken by Eugene's Voice and contains echoes of the Maiden and Man speech from Kaiser's *From Morn to Midnight*. "Maiden and man . . . fulness in the void," wrote Kaiser. "Maiden and man . . . the beginning and the end. Maiden and man . . . the seed and the flower. Maiden and man . . . sense and aim and goal!" [13] Rice begins with "You and I. . . . You and I Sophie" and goes on to "Alpha and Omega . . . the first and the last . . . the beginning and the end" (p. 131). As Sophie's nightmare continues, the voices grow louder and louder and she tries in vain to escape the pointing fingers. In desperation, she rushes out and throws herself in front of the phallic subway train. Clearly, then, as this brief analysis of the play's expressionistic techniques has revealed, *The Subway* owes as much to the gospel according to Freud as to the teachings of Marx.

Among Rice's more than thirty published plays there are other nonrealistic but not necessarily expressionist dramas, probably the best known of which is *Dream Girl* (1945). Yet greatly diluted expressionist elements can be found here and there among these works. For example, in act 1, scene 4, of *The Grand Tour* (1951) the protagonists speak and behave in a slightly stylized manner and one of them engages in audible thinking. The delivery room scene in *A New Life* (1943), which the playwright himself has called expressionistic,[14] in fact contains no grotesque distortions or even objectification, but it can be staged expressionistically, with a spotlight focused on the head of Edith Cleghorne as she is about to give birth to her baby. The hands of the attendants that emerge from the surrounding darkness recall the pointing fingers in the nightmare scene in *The Subway*. At the end of scene 1 of *Two on an Island* (1940) two New York taxi cabs collide, and the drivers begin to shout epithets at each other. As the sound of honking automobile horns increases, Rice's stage directions recall his handling of the turmoil in the mind of Zero when he murdered his boss. "The MEN are talking volubly and gesticulating violently, the radios are going full blast, and there is a swelling crescendo of automobile horns, radio cars, sirens, ambulance bells, and fire engine gongs, as the Curtain Falls." [15]

Two on an Island probably had its genesis in an unproduced and only partially published work called *The Sidewalks of New York* (written in 1925). Rice has stated that some of the scenes of this play "were realistic, some symbolic, some expressionistic." [16] Of the four published parts none can be termed truly expressionist. However, several of the unpublished scenes of *The Sidewalks of New York*, subtitled "A Play without Words"

(MS in the Library of Congress), contain distortions that objectify the characters' inner states—when a country girl dreams of faraway places, the rear wall of her room becomes transparent, revealing the silhouette of a great city (scene 1); when a nun desires a handsome young man, an erotic vision involving an archangel materializes on the stage (scene 9); when two lovers meet in a park, amorous pairs engage in a pagan orgy of sensual dancing to the music of Stravinsky's *Le Sacre du printemps* (scene 20).

In *The House in Blind Alley* (published in 1932), a dream fantasy involving Mother Goose and her children, Rice satirizes the expressionists' obsessive concern with subjective forces. As Jack the Giant Killer is beseeching the Man in the Moon to rescue Cinderella from the corporate giants of Janfirst and Julfirst, the Man in the Moon replies: "What does [her imprisonment] matter if her Ego is free? The body is nothing. The body does not exist. I deny its existence! The world does not exist. It is an illusion. Only the Ego exists. . . . As for your princess: Let her liberate her Ego." [17] Rice himself went a long way toward "liberating" and presenting in terms of visual stage reality the frail egos of Mr. Zero and Sophie Smith.

As the author of an article in the *Theatre Arts Monthly* pointed out in 1924, there were signs of a trend toward "a new kind of dramatic form . . . in which the movements taking place on the stage were felt quite naturally to be living projections of the movements of thought, will and feeling which take place inside a human personality." He concluded by noting that Elmer Rice's *The Adding Machine* "appears to be an actual attempt at the kind of projection I have suggested, and the movement called 'Expressionism' a conscious effort towards it." [18] The role of the Theatre Guild, which staged *The Adding Machine,* in promoting "the movement called Expressionism" will become even more evident when we consider the Guild's association with John Howard Lawson.

6

John Howard Lawson

When the Theatre Guild produced John Howard Law-son's *Processional* in 1925, the play impressed a number of viewers and reviewers and irritated many others. Letters attacking and defending the work were published in newspapers, and about two weeks after the opening of the play, the Guild scheduled a debate on it. The discussion was held at the Klaw Theatre and attracted an overflow crowd, forcing the Guild to make an apology in its next bulletin to those subscribers who could not find seats. According to the *New York Times* (February 2, 1925), "several hundred people, unable to enter the packed theatre, organized impromptu discussions in Forty-fifth Street." The debate, reported *The Theatre Guild Bulletin*, "was a most stimulating event." The leading opponent of *Processional* was John Anderson, the *New York Evening Post* drama critic. Elmer Rice defended the play. When members of the audience joined in the debate, most of them endorsed Mr. Rice's point of view. On the same day, an article appeared in the *New York Times Magazine*, castigating audiences for failing to recognize a true portrait of America in *Processional* and calling the play a "landmark" that reveals "how far . . . we have been engulfed on the cultural side in European influences."[1] A few days later a letter to the *Times* (February 8, 1925) suggested that "though he denies it, Mr. Lawson is undoubtedly writing after the manner of the German expressionists."

Like O'Neill and Rice, Lawson refused to acknowledge his debt to Continental expressionism. "When I wrote 'Roger Bloomer'," he explained in a letter to the *Times* (March 18, 1923) soon after the opening of that play, "I was amazed to find it described as 'expressionism'. I made a hasty canvass of my friends to find out what 'expressionism' was. Unfortunately, none of them knew, but I have learned enough about it to know that 'expressionism' has very rigorous laws and tenets of its own." *Roger Bloomer*, concludes Lawson, "cannot be judged by these standards, any more than by the standards of the conventional theatre." In conversation with the present writer, however, Lawson recalled having read at least some of the German dramatists, including Frank Wedekind, Walter Hasenclever, and Ernst Toller, and he singled out Henri-René Lenormand's *Failures* as the most important influence on *Roger Bloomer*.[2]

Lawson's initial contact with new developments in Continental drama can be traced to his participation in the First World War. Like a number of other American writers of his generation, including E. E. Cummings, Lawson had joined the war as an ambulance driver. After the Armistice, he remained in Paris, a city teeming with revolutionary ideas in art, literature, music, and the drama. John Dos Passos, another member of the ambulance corps, with whom Lawson attended Parisian cultural events, has written about the intellectual excitement of this period.

> We were hardly out of uniform before we were hearing the music of Stravinsky, looking at the paintings of Picasso and Juan Gris, standing in line for opening nights of Diaghilev's Ballet Russe. "Ulysses" had just been printed by Shakespeare and Company. Performances like "Noces" and "Sacre du Printemps" or Cocteau's "Mariés de la Tour Eiffel" were giving us a fresh notion of what might go on on the stage. We saw photographs of productions by Meyerhold and Piscator. In the motion pictures we were enormously stimulated by Eisenstein's "Cruiser Potemkin." [3]

Lawson, who had had two plays produced before he went to Europe, began *Roger Bloomer* in 1917 while in the ambulance corps and finished it in 1921 in Paris.

Roger Bloomer, which George Jean Nathan of the *American Mercury* (May 1926) called "an attempt to see New York through the eyes of a Georg Kaiser or Walter Hasenklever [sic]," depicts the spiritual journey of a midwestern youth who rebels against middle-class values and flees to the big city in search of maturity. The work has justifiably been compared to Wedekind's *Spring's Awakening* and Hasenclever's *The Son*,[4] but Roger and Louise are also distant, if rather coarse, cousins of the playwright and his Juliette (named simply He and She) in Lenormand's *Failures*, which Lawson remembers having seen in the company of John Dos Passos at least four or five times in Paris soon after the war. (The Guild produced *Failures* in November 1923.) The poverty-stricken protagonists in both *Failures* and *Roger Bloomer* stand out among other, more superficial characters as sensitive seekers for the meaning of life and love, and much of the action in both plays revolves around sexual matters. In *Failures* the down-and-out playwright kills Juliette, who has sold her body in order to supplement their meager income. When the police arrive, the playwright shoots himself, but not before he has talked about a better life in the next world. In *Roger Bloomer* Louise (who, according to a friend, is "no Juliet") commits suicide, having been driven to despair by money and sex. Implicated in her death, Roger is sent to prison, whence he emerges a spiritually reborn man. Structurally, both plays are episodic. *Failures* contains an effective scene of subjective distortion in which characters speak snippets of dialogue and move about in circles. A long nightmare concludes *Roger Bloomer*.

Lawson's play opens with the Bloomer family at dinner. The stage directions specify that they eat "with clock-like regularity,"[5] and the dialogue, as in the following exchange between the youth and his father, is frequently terse and interspersed with repetitions:

ROGER [*Embarrassed.*] But you have enough. . . .
I mean, you have money . . . enough money!
BLOOMER [*With almots passion.*] Never enough
money! Never enough. [P. 7]

The scene with the College Examiner, who sits on a
thronelike chair on a raised dais and in front of an enormous map of the United States, presents the protagonist's inner sensations rather than representing photographic surface reality. In New York, Roger finds himself in an office where five identical businessmen sit at
five identical desks and work in unison. As in the scene
in Elmer Rice's *The Adding Machine* in which the Boss
fires Mr. Zero, Roger hears only those words that capture
the spirit of the capitalistic system: "Six million . . . er
. . . marks, fourteen hundred thousand . . . er . . .
yen . . ." (p. 106). Later he meets a Ragged Man,
whose lines suggest that he might be Roger's alter ego.
At an exclusive club, Old Gentlemen comment on newspaper headlines ("Saloons, brothels, gambling dens,
tenements, crimes of passion" [p. 137]) —another device
for objectifying the thoughts of the protagonist.

When Roger, who has been jailed for a crime of
which he is innocent, lies down to sleep in act 3, "the
prison walls open" (p. 195), and his dream is presented
in the "technique of a very rapid ballet, with accompaniment of words half chanted" (p. 196). In this "nightmare of pursuit," played at great speed, characters who
have appeared earlier in the play change into grotesque
personifications of the "conventions and proprieties"
harassing Roger. In the second strophe of the dream,
Roger holds a large sword, with which he lunges at
various females. When he plunges it into a Street
Walker, she "starts to wriggle on it, . . . crooning las-
civiously" (p. 212). The sword then turns into a big
green snake. Behind this erotic façade lurks Death, but
in the final strophe the spirit of Roger's dead girl friend
Louise, representing the life force, offers him her support and leaves him "ready for manhood" (p. 196),

walking toward a symbolic bright ray of light from an open door. Several of the grotesque dream figures are masked, and the scene contains numerous distortions.

Except for a distorted view of the city on the painted drop curtain, the Equity Players' production of *Roger Bloomer* (March 1, 1923), was staged with more or less conventional scenery and proved unsuccessful. Lawson was able, however, to reopen the play two weeks later at the Greenwich Village Theatre, where black drapes and unrealistic, brightly painted cutouts effectively heightened the expressionistic dramaturgy of the play. The remounted production also cut down on the number of properties, as, for example, in the college examination scene, where an ordinary stepladder was substituted for the raised seat of the Examiner. Yet even before these changes were made, John Corbin of the *New York Times* (March 11, 1923) declared the Equity production of *Roger Bloomer* to be "by far the most complete and technically perfect example of dramatic expressionism that has yet reached us." Other reviewers were intrigued by the interplay of lights and shadows, which reminded them of the visual effects in *The Cabinet of Dr. Caligari.* Lawson told the present writer that he thinks he saw *Caligari* in Paris, though he is not absolutely certain of that. Yet wherever he did see it, he added, this expressionist film impressed him greatly.

In act 2 of *Roger Bloomer* Louise offers to get Roger a job in her office. To his question, "Why should you do that?" she replies, "Them that seen despair together must stand by each other. You must come, get in the crowd, get in the subway, get in the procession" (p. 103). It is precisely this feeling of camaraderie under extremely adverse conditions that unites the proletarian hero and his girl in Lawson's *Processional,* a play on which he had been at work in Paris while writing *Roger Bloomer* and which the Theatre Guild produced on January 12, 1925.

With *Processional*—his best-known work—Lawson abandoned the complete reliance on expressionistic dramaturgy that characterizes *Roger Bloomer*. "I have endeavored to create," he wrote in the preface to the published play, "a method which shall express the American scene in native idiom, a method as far removed from the older realism as from the facile mood of Expressionism." He goes on to refer to "this new technique" as being "essentially vaudevillesque in character" and having a "staccato, burlesque" rhythm, "carried out by a formalized arrangement of jazz music." [6] Yet the play contains numerous expressionistic elements.

Processional presents the agon of Dynamite Jim, a young striker at a West Virginia coal mine, and the forces of capitalism. The latter are represented by grotesquely exaggerated characters. Jim escapes from jail, kills a soldier, and seeks refuge with his mother, only to leave in disgust when he learns that she has sold herself to soldiers. In this scene, entitled "Mother and Son," Lawson again introduces a character who reads newspaper headlines, and Old Maggie, Jim's grandmother, dies when she overhears the truth about her daughter's conduct, thus suggesting a parallel with the grandmother in Kaiser's *From Morn to Midnight*, who dies when the Cashier's lust-inspired actions upset the everyday routine of their middle-class household.

The brief scene entitled "The Man Hunt," during which Jim is captured by the soldiers, is thoroughly expressionistic. Against an aural background of "drum beats and rapid rhythm of music" (p. 170), the Man in Silk Hat, who could have stepped down from Lyonel Feininger's 1910 expressionist painting "Uprising," comments on the action through a megaphone in characteristically terse language: "Stop him . . . he's in the field . . . hunted he runs . . . Halt! . . . Shoot! . . . The Man Hunt!" (p. 171). Jim is caught by the seat of his pants on a point of a nine-foot-high iron fence. As the soldiers close in on him, Lawson's stage directions underscore the nightmare quality of the scene: "A flashlight [is] turned on JIM where he hangs sprawling in the air, a figure of grotesque defeat. Points of guns bristle in a circle round him on the edge of the light. Blare of music" (p. 172). In the last act the mutilated hero marries Sadie, who carries his child, in a jazz wedding. Like Edmund Wilson's *The Crime in the Whistler Room*, Lawson's early plays conclude on a note of hope, reminiscent of a number of German expressionist dramas that proclaimed the coming of the utopian New Man. In the nightmare scene in *Roger Bloomer* the spirit of Louise chases away the obscene Old Women by saying, "Away, ghosts of yesterday, for the young are coming marching, marching; can't you hear the echo of their feet, can't you hear them singing a new song?" (p. 222). In *Processional* Sadie's optimistic curtain line, "I'm agonna raise my kid, sing to him soft . . ." (p. 218), strongly suggests an ideological affinity between Lawson and the German expressionists. It was no doubt this quality in *Processional*, coupled with its expressionistic techniques, that caused Eugene O'Neill to refer to it as "too much German patent American goods." [7] Several reviewers pointed out the play's affinity with the *Caligari* film, and Robert Littell, who sided with John Anderson in attacking the play at the time of the Theatre Guild debate on *Processional*, discussed the work in the *New Republic* (January 28, 1925) in terms of an "orchestra of methods," which included "comico-realistic expressionism," "social-comment expressionism," and "American-comment burlesque expressionism."

Lawson's next work, *Nirvana* (Greenwich Village Theatre, March 3, 1926), begins quite realistically in the office of Dr. Alonzo Weed. Yet the opening stage directions, "On the darkened stage the violet light of an X-ray apparatus buzzes startlingly," [8] suggest the possibility of latent expressionism in the work. This promise is partially fulfilled in act 2, where such caricatured types as a Giggling Girl and a Drunken Man attend a nightmarish party. Music is used to give rhythm to the scene, and when the Tall Man spills a drink on a lady's gown, he wipes her dress with a large handkerchief, while the Hungry Girl has "her mouth full of sandwiches which she is eating rapidly" (p. II–2). The effect thus produced is an accurate presentation of an intoxicated person's perception of the festivities around him. Lawson distorts reality also in act 3, where an operation is conducted in "staccato medical pantomime" in a room that is described as "shadowy and unreal" (p. III–1). To this play, according to Lawson, O'Neill acknowledged a debt when writing *Dynamo*. Reuben Light in the O'Neill play and Bill Weed in *Nirvana* are both searching for a new religion, and when Bill speaks of "an electromagnetic Christ" (p. III–10) and of building "a high altar where the spark of power lies in perpetual vibration" (p. III–25), parallels between the two plays become obvious.

After the failure of *Nirvana*, Lawson joined a group of young dramatists to form the New Playwrights' Theatre. Their first production, on March 2, 1927, was Lawson's *Loud Speaker*. The playwright has called it "a political farce with a constructivist setting," [9] for Lawson and his colleagues were at that time corresponding with Russian constructivist Vsevolod Meyerhold as well as with Erwin Piscator, the father of epic theatre. In the introduction to the printed play, Joseph Wood Krutch talks about the play's *commedia dell' arte* quality.[10] A more accurate description of *Loud Speaker* has been given by Malcolm Goldstein, who somewhat speciously recognizes the epic quality of the play: "Lawson's inspiration was Russian, not German, but he seems in this play to have been more Brechtian than Bertolt Brecht himself in his attempt to 'alienate' his patrons." [11] Lawson apparently arrived at his epic techniques independently of Brecht's work, for he does not remember having heard of Brecht until several years after his association with the New Playwrights' Theatre. (And when Mordecai Gorelik published an annotated version of some of Brecht's *Threepenny Opera* notes in *Theatre Workshop* in 1937, Lawson, in a letter to that journal [no. 4, 1937], attacked Brecht's idea "that dramas may be divorced from emotion.") Both playwrights, however, were influenced in their search for a more effective dramatic form by the same theatrical conventions—expressionism, constructivism, and epic theatre.

Lawson talks about his pursuit of the proper technique in a letter he wrote to Gilbert W. Gabriel soon after the production of *Nirvana* (March 8, 1926; in Lawson papers). "You see," confesses Lawson, "I'm still feeling my way toward some sort of form." He states that he "could not rest upon the spectacular and uncertain method of 'Processional' without experimenting in another and even more difficult direction," and though the letter goes on to refer to his basically expressionistic technique of "dramatizing states of mind and mental stress" in *Nirvana,* in execution this method produced stylized but not consistently expressionistic results. Lawson refers to his method as "a sort of ritualistic technique" and points out that while "being far from pure realism," it "runs the risk of being mistaken for just a horribly bad realistic play." Both *Nirvana* and *Loud Speaker* were regarded by most critics as being just that, whereas the plays actually reflect an attempt on Lawson's part to move away from expressionism without embracing realism.

Nevertheless, there are unmistakable traces of expressionism in *Loud Speaker.* The characters are either easily recognizable types (the politician, the neglected wife, the hard-boiled flapper, the tabloid reporter) or are identified merely by their occupations or appearances (e.g., Maid, First Photographer, Bearded Stranger). The scenes are short. The language is frequently ecstatic and disconnected. And distortions are used to convey the essence of a situation by means of visual objectification. For example, as Harry U. Collins begins to address his election committee, it is revealed to consist of "two dummies with wax business faces" (p. 19). Similarly, the Harlem delegation is made up of six masked Negro politicians "of exaggerated type" (p. 75). The end of the play finds Collins in the governor's mansion as flag-waving figures with wax faces throng around him. Robert Benchley, reviewing *Loud Speaker* in *Life* (March 24, 1927), called it "the first expressionistic play in which the hero is not crushed to death by the Futility of Modern Civilization."

In *Loud Speaker*, Collins's daughter elopes with a newspaper reporter to China. Much of the action of Lawson's next play, *The International*, which the New Playwrights produced on January 12, 1928, takes place in Tibet, where David, the son of an American financier, finds adventure with Alise, a pretty Soviet secret agent. Like *Processional* and *Loud Speaker*, *The International* employs jazz rhythms and chants. The setting, writes Lawson in the production notes, is to be structural, consisting of "separate massive and strangely shaped geometric blocks" that are connected by means of stairs and slopes.[12] The characters are two-dimensional, most of the scenes shift quickly, and the choral interludes, one of which features masked Tibetan dancers, are highly stylized.

In the second brothel scene of the play, Lawson objectifies by means of dancing and chanting the transformation of Freudian impulses into Marxist ones. "We are the ground that got no seed. . . . We are the field that got no plow," chant the two choruses. "The plow is a sword!" replies Alise, to which the Negro prostitute adds, "Open to the sword, take me shiny sword . . . Plow sword. . . . Plow!" At this point, with the full chorus kneeling, Alise "holds up a sword with a ragged red flag tied to it" (pp. 224, 227).

In a recent study of Lawson's plays, Gerald Rabkin contends that Lawson's "intellectual ambivalence" destroys the "artistic coherence" of *The International*, for although "the symbolic transference of the sexual sword into the revolutionary sword might well have been a coherent metaphor with which to order the disparate elements" of the play, "the Freudian serpent conquers the Marxian sword" as Alise "exchanges her political principles for David's love."[13] This criticism warms over Michael Gold's attack on Lawson in the

New Masses (April 10, 1934), in which Gold accused Lawson of being ideologically confused and charged that "the futile hero and his Communist heroine" in *The International* come out of the revolutionary conflict "singing a musical comedy love-duet that consoles them." However, an examination of the dramaturgy of the last act of *The International* reveals neither ideological ambivalence nor artistic incoherence. On the contrary, Lawson's development of the central metaphor is quite consistent.

It is true that at the beginning of the act Alise wavers somewhat in her revolutionary faith because of physical fear, yet when David speaks of love, she answers, "It's no time for that" (p. 234). "If you want me," she goes on, "you must lie on the breasts of guns" (p. 240). When David asks her how she got the scars on her hands, the action shifts to Italy. This expressionistic memory scene involving Alise's encounter with Aretini, a Fascist officer, explains her momentary "sword-point sharp" fear, the scars, and her steely determination to remain faithful to the revolutionary movement.

The scene then shifts to the nightmare brothel where a Negro prostitute has strangled a financier. When Alise asks what made her do it, the Negress replies, "You did" (p. 260). Coming immediately after Alise's declaration that she has "many hands, many voices" (p. 259), this shifting of responsibility in the death of a capitalist from the prostitute to the revolutionary is obviously symbolic. To make the point even clearer in visual terms, Lawson makes Alise stand at the highest point of the constructivist stage, disheveled, her arms raised as shafts of light focus on her "from all points in the darkness" (p. 264). Her cry of "our brothers in the sky, join us" is a variation upon the theme of "Workers of the world, unite!"

In the last scene David and Alise huddle beneath a barricade. When David wonders, "Have we been wrong?" she answers, "No," adding, "We are alone here, but don't forget . . . Karneski is leading the hordes of Asia!"(pp. 273, 274). Yielding to the fatally wounded David's feverish pleading of "Say love," Alise "uncertainly" speaks that word. Behind her the chorus intones, "Dead but not at rest . . . waitin' to rise" (p. 276). David's body goes limp in Alise's embrace, and the curtain comes down as a shot rings out, killing Alise's last companion. If anything is going to rear its head, it will be the spirit of Marxist revolution ("Dead but not at rest . . . waitin' to rise") and not Dr. Rabkin's Freudian snake. Lawson's own evaluation of his dramatic mode in *The International* was expressed in a letter to the drama editor of the *New York Times* (January 29, 1928), in which the playwright criticized a reviewer who had referred to "the dying state" of the expressionist mode. "It would seem apparent to any bystander," insisted Lawson in defending *The International*, that expressionism "is giving boisterous indications of young but lusty vitality."

In 1933 Lawson called *The International* (which reminded a German commentator on the New Playwrights' Theatre of the expressionist dramas of Arnolt Bronnen) [14] "the most interesting and significant experiment in form and content which I have attempted." [15] Soon he was to turn to the realistic mode. Yet he revealed his experimental past with the unrealistic sets and cinematically changing scenes of *The Pure in Heart* (1934) as well as with the occasional touches of stylization and suggestions of nightmarish settings in *Marching Song* (1937). In 1961 he rewrote the realistic, unpublished *Parlor Magic* into a work that makes use of film interludes to objectify the thoughts of the characters. This play has been produced in the Soviet Union and in East Germany, but not in the United States.

The termination of Lawson's experimental phase roughly coincides with the closing of the New Playwrights' Theatre, which produced his *Loud Speaker* and *The International*. Like these imaginative works, most of the other plays staged by the New Playwrights contain expressionist elements.

7

The New Playwrights' Theatre

John Howard Lawson was but one of the five experimental dramatists who organized the New Playwrights' Theatre in the winter of 1926–27. The others were Em Jo Basshe, John Dos Passos, Francis Edwards Faragoh, and Michael Gold. While the critic Alexander Woollcott dubbed them the "revolting playwrights," the *New York Times* (February 7, 1927) called the founders of the new theatre "recognized . . . advocates of the so-called 'expressionistic drama.' " Dos Passos, who died recently, is well known as a novelist. Mike Gold, longtime editor of *New Masses* and champion of proletarian literature, died in 1967. Em Jo Basshe, like Gold, had been associated with the Provincetown Players, who produced his expressionistic *Adam Solitaire* in 1925. He died in 1939. Before joining the New Playwrights, Francis Edwards Faragoh (died in 1966) had been drama editor of *Pearson's Magazine* and had translated Lajos Egri's expressionistic *Rapid Transit*. All five had had plays produced prior to the New Playwrights venture.

Most of the practical work involved in organizing the New Playwrights' Theatre was done by Mike Gold. The artistic pacesetter, however, was Lawson (and not Dos Passos as a recent study of the New Playwrights has rather unconvincingly tried to establish).[1] Lawson's views on "the new theatre" were published in several New York newspapers as well as in the *Pinwheel* playbill of the Neighborhood Playhouse (season 1926–27, no. 4). Entitled "The New Showmanship," his article announced that the aim of the young playwrights was to return to "the art of telling a story" and "putting a spectacle or series of events before a crowd." "Dynamic" and "pictorial," said Lawson, were the adjectives that best suggested the qualities that characterize not only the new mode of writing but all good drama, which excluded, of course, the current fare "in the flesh marts and sombre commercial temples of Broadway." And expressionism—contrary to popular opinion—was able to provide "dynamic movement" and "visual effectiveness." In a thumbnail history of the new movement, Lawson mentioned Ernst Toller's *Man and the Masses*, Henri-René Lenormand's *The Failures*, and Georg Kaiser's *From Morn to Midnight*, and labeled O'Neill's *The Hairy Ape*, Rice's *The Adding Machine*, and his own *Roger Bloomer* their American equivalents. The new mode, he insisted in the words of Continental expressionist theoreticians, gave him as a playwright "his opportunity . . . to catch the very essence and stir of actuality."

Influenced by expressionist theory as well as by the production methods of constructivism and epic theatre, the New Playwrights issued in the *New York Times* of February 27, 1927, an Artaudesque manifesto proclaiming "a theatre where the spirit, the movement, the music of this age is carried on, accentuated, amplified, crystallized. A theatre which shocks, terrifies, matches wits with the audience. . . . In all, a theatre which is as drunken, as barbaric, as clangorous as our age." The choice of adjectives in this outburst of radical sentiments mirrored the tone of the exhibits on display at the International Theatre Exposition, held in New York in February and March of 1926 under the auspices of the Theatre Guild, the Provincetown Players, the Greenwich Village Theatre, and the Neighborhood Playhouse. Among the Russian exhibits were items relating to Meyerhold's theatre and Tairov's staging of *Phaedra* at the famed Kamerny. The German contribution included photographs of a production of Toller's *Transformation* (*Die Wandlung*, 1919), an expressionist stage for Kaiser's *Gas* (which had just been produced at the Goodman Theatre in Chicago), and designer Hans Strohbach's work for Toller's *Man and the Masses*. Among the American designers who participated were Boris Aronson with David Pinski's *The Final Balance*; Mordecai Gorelik with Lawson's *Processional*, Karel Čapek's *R.U.R.*, and Leonid Andreyev's *King Hunger*; Robert Edmond Jones with expressionist settings for John Alden Carpenter's ballet *Skyscrapers*; Donald Oenslager with Andreyev's *The Life of Man*; and Cleon Throckmorton with several plays, including O'Neill's *The Emperor Jones* and *The Hairy Ape*. According to Lawson, the impact of the exposition on him and his soon-to-be colleagues at the New Playwrights' Theatre was tremendous.[2]

The winter 1926 issue of *The Little Review*, devoted entirely to the International Theatre Exposition, contains excerpts from an article, "The American Stage: Reflections of an Amateur," by Otto Kahn, in which the banker and patron of the arts indulged in "the hope that there may be, in the not too distant future, at least one theatre in New York, devoted exclusively to youth — a stage where young America shall have its innings." Kahn's hopes were realized within a year by the founding of the New Playwrights' Theatre, for which he himself provided an endowment.

Most of the plays the New Playwrights produced in addition to Lawson's *Loud Speaker* and *The International* (discussed in the previous chapter) contain expressionistic elements. In the group's second production (following *Loud Speaker*), Em Jo Basshe's Negro drama *Earth* (March 9, 1927), there is chanting and voodoo dancing to the accompaniment of a tom-tom, and when Brother Eliah announces the coming of the Lord to sit in judgment on Sister Deborah, "the stage is flooded with the kind of light appropriate to the representation of the vision in the minds of the characters."[3] Though

the vision itself does not materialize, the action of *Earth*
takes place not so much in a recognizable geographical
region as in the playwright's mind.

Basshe's second offering, *The Centuries*[4] (November
29, 1927), a kaleidoscopic picture of Jewish immigrant
life in New York, is considerably more experimental in
form and involves abbreviated dialogue, machine sounds,
feverish activity, and the objectification of subjective
states. His *Adam Solitaire* (discussed in Chapter Four)
as well as his published plays, *Invitation* (1928), *Snick-
ering Horses* (1938), and *Doomsday Circus* (1938), contain a wide spectrum of expressionist elements. The
most spectacular of these are to be found in the last-
mentioned work, in which capitalistic America emerges
as a gigantic circus. A Chairman of the Board assumes
the role of the ringmaster, who brandishes a whip, and
at the end of the play a ticker, reminiscent of Elmer
Rice's adding machine, produces enough tape to envelop
the entire stage.

The second season of the New Playwrights' Theatre
opened on October 19, 1927, with Paul Sifton's *The
Belt*. The play (with settings by Dos Passos) deals with
workers in an automobile plant. When the Old Man, a
caricature of Henry Ford, tries to shut down the factory,
the workers revolt and destroy the assembly line—The
Belt—in a scene that is somewhat reminiscent of Toller's
The Machine Wreckers (*Die Maschinenstürmer*, 1922).
The Belt is on the whole quite realistic, but Sifton establishes a charged atmosphere with these opening stage
directions: "The distant hum of The Belt seems to form
a continuous curtain against which the Act is played.
Talk is carried on in high, strained tones, rising frequently to sudden peaks of shouts and screeching."[5]
When Bill Vance, a young laborer, finally admits that
he, too, feels tired after a grueling day on the assembly
line, Sifton objectifies his thoughts by revealing The
Belt behind an inner curtain. As a procession of automobile frames moves slowly across the stage, men cluster
around it, working "monotonously" (p. 67).

Of Sifton's later plays, 1931– (written with his wife Claire and produced by the Group Theatre in December 1931) is another mildly expressionistic social protest play. Its structure is episodic; the characters are one-dimensional; the dialogue is often terse and repetitious; the protagonist engages in disconnected monologues; and the grotesquely distorted setting reveals the anxieties of unemployed workers: a factory gate with a "No Help Wanted" sign on it grows larger and larger—while the signs multiply—until the gate looks "like the entrance to a great fortress." [6]

The last production of the New Playwrights' second season—following Lawson's *The International*—was Michael Gold's constructivist/expressionist *Hoboken Blues* (February 17, 1928), which undoubtedly owes a debt to Gold's contact with Meyerhold's theatre during a visit to Moscow in 1925. Set in Harlem and Hoboken, the play calls for futurist settings; "It would be a calamity to treat the scenes in the play realistically," writes Gold in the opening stage directions.[7] After the relatively realistic first act, Sam Pickens, an unemployed Negro, arrives in Hoboken to look for a job. The setting for this act, specifies Gold, must be "a composite of all that goes on in SAM PICKENS' mind" and suggest a "battle of jungle and modern industrialism" (p. 584).

Having failed in several attempts to hold a menial job while being abused by grotesque figures wearing white masks, Sam accepts a position in a sideshow booth that features the popular sport of "Hit the Nigger and Get a Cigar." A sailor scores a bull's eye. Once more Sam relinquishes a job. Considerably shaken by this experience, he encounters a circus, several members of which resemble his friends from act 1, with the whitemasked Ringmaster looking like the rich undertaker who has been wooing his wife. As the circus leaves, four masked policemen "stalk up in unison" (p. 590) and kick Sam in the head. This gives the playwright further opportunity to objectify the protagonist's inner state and his hatred of modern industrialism. In the last act Sam returns to a nightmarish and jazzed-up Harlem, shakes off his dream and pleads for tolerance and a universal brotherhood of "poor men, black and white . . . where no one is hungry, where no one is lynched, where dere's no money or bosses" (p. 626).

A more militant approach to world brotherhood is to be found in novelist Upton Sinclair's *Singing Jailbirds*, the first production (December 4, 1928) of the New Playwrights' third—and final—season. Most of Sinclair's numerous plays are traditional in form, but an interesting forerunner of *Singing Jailbirds* is *Hell* (published in 1923), which H. L. Mencken categorized with the dramatic "novelties" from central Europe, and which O'Neill thought "would be extremely interesting for [the Provincetown Players] to attempt." [8] In *Hell* Sinclair calls for film projections to give visual form to what is narrated in blank verse and at times has the characters abandon their roles and become actors chatting about their work and criticizing the play.

Singing Jailbirds, like Toller's *Transformation* or *Man and the Masses*, alternates realistic scenes with the visions of the protagonist, who has been jailed for his activities as a labor leader. In the trial scene, the judge appears as a snarling tiger, a witness as a snake, the defense attorney as a jack-in-the-box, and the clerk as a rat. "The whole scene," writes Sinclair in the stage directions, "is played fast and wild, it being not a natural scene, but a delirium." [9] Under Em Jo Basshe's direction, *Singing Jailbirds* was staged with masks and grossly distorted sets and had the longest run of the plays presented by the New Playwrights' Theatre. As John Dos Passos later pointed out in a *New Masses* article (August 1929), the popular success of Sinclair's play was due to the fact that the staging "did not depart too far from the methods of expressionism with which [the audiences] were already familiar." According to the *New York Times* review (December 5, 1928), "The mechanical trick [of representing the visions] was, indeed, much better turned . . . than it was by the Theatre Guild in

'Masse Mensch' and other imported things of that sort."
O'Neill was deeply moved by the play; the English
novelist Israel Zangwill called it "one of [Sinclair's]
greatest artistic successes," confessing that the work "almost converts me to expressionistic drama"; and Floyd
Dell, in his study of Sinclair, refers to *Singing Jailbirds*
as "a more poignant and effective example of the expressionistic drama than any that has been produced on
the American stage." In the spring of 1928 Erwin Piscator produced it in Berlin.[10]

No expressionist plays by the two remaining founders
of the New Playwrights' Theatre, John Dos Passos and
Francis Edwards Faragoh, were staged by the group,
which gave Dos Passos's *Airways, Inc.* but nothing by
Faragoh. However, one earlier play by each of these
writers is thoroughly expressionistic. Dos Passos's *The
Garbage Man* (staged in the spring of 1925 by the Har-
vard Dramatic Club under the title *The Moon Is a
Gong*) received a New York production (again as *The
Moon Is a Gong*) on March 12, 1926, at the Cherry
Lane Playhouse, which was soon to house the New
Playwright's Theatre.

Dos Passos's play objectifies the inner world of two
young lovers, Tom and Jane, who are haunted by Death
in various guises, including that of a Garbage Man with
a "chalky and skull-like" face.[11] In the eight scenes of
The Garbage Man the playwright looks at the world
through the eyes of the main characters. For example,
at her mother's funeral, Jane's gossipy relatives, like
those in Andreyev's *The Life of Man*, appear as grotesquely drawn caricatures who dance around the coffin,
waiting for the minister to arrive. He fox-trots in, followed by some more waltzing next of kin. In another
scene the violence and horror of a train accident are
heightened by a distorted setting of railroad tracks, tele-
graph poles, and wrecking cranes that appears "livid
with the violent green glare of oxi-acetylene torches" (p.
51). This background clearly suggests the shakeup in
the lives of the protagonists, for in this scene Jane leaves
Tom.

Part 2 of *The Garbage Man* is a grotesquely distorted vision of modern America, not unlike that revealed in *Manhattan Transfer*. Speaking of his early novels in a *New York Times* article (October 25, 1959), Dos Passos admitted that his "excitement over the 'expressionist' theatre of the Nineteen-twenties had a good deal to do with shaping their style." Scene 2 of part 2 of *The Garbage Man* is an anxiety dream, in which Death appears, merrily "rolling a garbage can before him" (p. 124). When the Man in the Stovepipe Hat attempts to arrest Tom, the young man jumps on a fire escape, climbs to the roof, and disappears with policemen in pursuit. The episode ends with the giggling Garbage Man carrying off Jane. Purified by death, Tom and Jane begin their lives anew in the next scene. Dos Passos objectifies the birth of his New Man by confronting Tom and Jane with an expanse of starry blue sky.

Joseph Wood Krutch, writing in the *Nation* (March 31, 1926), was not far from the truth when he described the play as being "cast into the most extreme of expressionistic forms." In a letter to the present writer (September 5, 1966), Dos Passos speaks of his indebtedness to Continental sources: "We were all very much influenced by expressionistic developments in Europe. . . . I saw a couple of plays by Andreyev in translation, but in my case I suspect that the Diaghilev ballet was the great influence." Like Lawson and other American playwrights of the 1920s, Dos Passos was drawn not only to the avant-garde drama of Europe but also to the new developments in music and the dance. Hence the introduction of jazz and choreography into such plays as Lawson's *Processional*, Wilson's *The Crime in the Whistler Room*, Gold's *Hoboken Blues*, and Dos Passos's *The Garbage Man*.

Jazz-vaudeville elements are prominent also in Francis Edwards Faragoh's *Pinwheel*, whose production at the Neighborhood Playhouse on February 3, 1927, caused what one newspaper termed "The Civil War Between the Expressionists." Along with the Provincetown Players and the Theatre Guild (formerly the Washington

Square Players), the Neighborhood Playhouse was known for its productions of experimental plays, including those by Andreyev and Lenormand. As early as 1921 this East Side group parodied the new scenic mode by inserting into their production of Calthorp and Granville-Barker's *The Harlequinade* an episode involving a Bronx Art Theatre of the future, which eliminated the actors and left the action to the lights, music, and scenery.

Faragoh's *Pinwheel* seems to have been inspired by John Alden Carpenter's jazz-ballett *Skyscrapers*, which was danced at the Metropolitan Opera House in 1926 (and which, in turn, owes something to Diaghilev's Ballets Russes). The play opens on "a crosscut" of New York, which is not to be "a definite, identifiable section of the city," but rather "the tangible essence of the metropolis," [12] and objectifies the internal states of a "Jane" and her "Guy." On her way to work in a hurrying procession of "standardized" subway commuters, The Jane meets The Guy. Faragoh objectifies her subjective reactions to The Guy's behavior in terms of concrete stage reality, for when he asks her to slow down and talk to him, voices repeat the one word that is uppermost in her mind at that moment, "Late . . . late . . . late . . . laattte . . . " (p. 12). When he "gets fresh," she runs away from him. The chase and capture of The Jane are reflected in the movements of the pleasure-seeking Coney Island crowd. In a dance hall, dominated by two gigantic Negro saxophone players, the thoughts of the two lovers are objectified by means of rhymed, lyric dialogue.

The office where The Jane works is dominated by an enormous typewriter, reminiscent of Lee Simonson's huge adding machine in the last act of Elmer Rice's play. The manager's dictation is terse and disconnected: "Messrs . . . Yours of even date . . . Shipment of linoleum, coffins, carpet-tacks, kerosene, diapers, lamps, sausages . . . *His voice trails off, although he still pantomimes dictation. The girls go through the motions of*

typing, noiselessly now" (p. 35). When The Jane goes
with her latest conquest to the movies (the figures on
the screen, writes Faragoh, should appear "unreal and
grotesque" [p. 43]), she again voices her thoughts, as did
Sophie in Rice's *The Subway,* and her subconscious wish
to play opposite the handsome screen idol is objectified
in the next scene, where The Jane takes part in the action on the screen. This episode is played behind a gauze
curtain, and Faragoh calls for the use of a strobe light.
In part 4, The Jane spends an expressionistic night in a
cabaret with a Sugar Daddy, "a caricature of his type"
(p. 102). Here the stage directions call for a grotesquely
distorted "Night on Broadway," during which the protagonist engages in an orgiastic shopping spree.

Most reviewers found *Pinwheel* weak but praised the
production and almost to a man labeled the work expressionistic, relating it to earlier plays in the same mode.
"With the possible exception of the Theatre Guild's
'Processional,'" declared Joseph Wood Krutch in the
Nation (February 23, 1927), "no piece in a similar genre
has been done so well in New York." John Mason
Brown, writing in *Theatre Arts* (April 1927), agreed
that many of the "limping moments" of the play "have
been faked into a dynamic theatricality." He singled out
the cabaret scene, in which "the prosy course of telegraphic brevity that haunts the dialogue is . . . glossed
over by the direction, which, by the arrangement of the
players, the timing of the Jane's speeches, as compared
to the timing and motions of the dancers, manages to
give the entire incident a subtle, contrapuntal rhythm
that sends it syncopating to its climax."

Lawson, however, found fault with the Neighborhood
Playhouse production of *Pinwheel.* It was too expressionistic, he felt, and did not follow the realistic spirit of
the play. After communicating his views in a personal
letter to Alice Lewisohn, who had directed Faragoh's
play, Lawson published a letter in the *New York Sun*
(February 12, 1927). He criticized the pacing of the action, the "shockingly stylized costumes," and the "curi-

ously forced behavior" of the actors. Claiming that *Pin-wheel* deals with "real" people, Lawson insisted that "Faragoh has put the flesh and blood of New York into a play." He then cited the Coney Island scene (which had suggested to Krutch "the enthusiastic imagination of a German who has read all the books published about America in Berlin"): "A fellow and his jane escape from the steaming sidewalks to fall in love among the freaks and hot dog venders" and asked, "Is that so aesthetical and expressionistic?" Coming so soon after "The New Showmanship," the article in which he had championed expressionism (and which was published in the playbill for the very same production of *Pinwheel*), Lawson's statements appear contradictory. However, in view of his own development from the pure expressionism of *Roger Bloomer* toward what might be termed an epic style in *Nirvana* and *Loud Speaker* (produced a month after *Pinwheel*), these pronouncements probably reflected Lawson's changing aesthetic beliefs.

Miss Lewisohn answered Lawson's charge with an offer that the New Playwrights put on a better production of *Pinwheel*. The challenge was accepted, and Lawson wrote a letter to the drama desk of the *New York Evening Post* (March 4, 1927), restating his objections to the Lewisohn production. Meanwhile the *Herald Tribune* (February 6, 1927) had carried an article which suggested that the playwright was unhappy with the Neighborhood Playhouse production. As the subtitle of the newspaper article proclaimed, "Francis Edwards Faragoh Dreamed That His Script Was Abandoned Entirely to Make a Scenic Holiday." However, Faragoh's own statement in the *Evening Post* (February 19, 1927) clearly indicates that he disagreed with Lawson's diagnosis of the play. *Pinwheel*, said its author, "is far less a drama of two people, or of a given set of characters, than a rapid-patterned dance of multitudes to the music of a gigantic hurdy-gurdy of steel and concrete." In keeping with expressionist theory, Faragoh denied that the characters were intended to be "real." Instead, they "serve more as illustrations, mouthpieces or even props." "They are types," he went on, "the stock products of a city and that city's civilization and philosophy." " 'Pinwheel,' in trying to be New York," he added, repeating his stage directions that so firmly establish his expressionistic orientation, "is not a single, definite, identifiable portion of the city, but a focusing, a tangible presentation of its essence."

The New Playwrights never did present *Pinwheel.* Yet Faragoh's play kept making news. On February 13 the *Herald Tribune* featured a picture of Dorothy Sands in the role of The Jane and noted that " 'Pinwheel' is proving to be a tumultuous entertainment." Two weeks later (February 27) the same newspaper focused attention on the *Pinwheel* controversy in an article on dramatic expressionism and reported that Faragoh's play was disowned by Lawson for "committing the mortal sin of dullness." Lawson may have thought the play dull, but the controversy over the Neighborhood Playhouse production of *Pinwheel* stirred up enough interest for Richard Watts of the *Herald Tribune* to devote several columns of the theatre section on Sunday, March 13, 1927, to an article he titled "Considering the Civil War Between the Expressionists."

Like everyone else at the time, Watts failed to notice the subtle change in Lawson's allegiance from expressionism to something approximating epic dramaturgy. Referring to Lawson as the high priest of the expressionists' cult, Watts agreed with him that the tempo of Miss Lewisohn's production had indeed been wrong, but he then went on to attack Faragoh's play as well as Lawson's own *Loud Speaker.* Lawson's second thoughts on Faragoh's play were published in 1936 in his *Theory and Technique of Playwriting,* in which he restored *Pinwheel* to its rightful place among expressionist plays.

According to a letter Mike Gold sent to Otto Kahn, *Pinwheel* was to be staged "next season by the Reinhardt theatre in Vienna." [13] That production seems not to have materialized either. Perhaps we can find a clue to the commercial failure not only of *Pinwheel* but most other experimental plays of the decade in Dos Passos's fictional musings about the state of the American theatre in the 1920s.

> Crowds, he noticed, gaylooking crowds were pouring into the Greenwich Village Theatre. They looked better dressed than his audience at the Miniature. They looked richer, the girls looked prettier. A speakeasy crowd laughing and giggling as they shoved toward the box office to buy their seats. *Village Frolics*. A damn fool musical show . . . People pouring into a girl and music show instead of going to see something that would make them understand.[14]

The decade of the 1920s was indeed a great era for revues; it was the golden age of Florenz Ziegfeld and his *Follies*. Commercial Broadway produced, furthermore, a flood of sentimental operettas, which John Mason Brown called "molasses set to music." And *Abie's Irish Rose*, of course, had the longest run of the decade. For not only the public, but many critics preferred such fare to thought-provoking expressionist works. To Robert A. Parker of the *Independent*, for example, Zelda Sears's musical comedy *The Clinging Vine* seemed "as respectable a contribution to the American Theatre as 'The Adding Machine'—and a dozen times more entertaining" (April 14, 1923). Yet the new spirit in the drama, Belasco's "cubism of the theater—the wail of the incompetent and the degenerate," managed to invade the citadel of the American commercial theatre. For in the 1920s expressionism succeeded in establishing a considerable bridgehead even on Broadway.

8

Broadway and Beyond

The extent to which the "cubism of the theater" that irritated Belasco had penetrated the sedate world of middleclass theatregoers is revealed by a feuilleton entitled "Expressionism" that appeared midway through the decade in the stately *Independent* (April 18, 1925). The author of this light piece of fiction attempts to laugh at the undefinable nature of the new dramatic mode but in doing so reveals its impact on the art of the day. For by 1925 even Broadway theatregoers, who shunned the hard benches at the Provincetown Playhouse or scorned the experimental bills of the Theatre Guild, could no longer avoid contact with expressionistic dramaturgy, which had been thoroughly commercialized by George S. Kaufman and Marc Connelly when their successful *Beggar on Horseback*, ridiculing American businessmen's lack of culture, opened in 1924.

An adaptation of a German play, *Beggar on Horseback* arrived on Broadway nine years after the founding of the Provincetown Players and four years after O'Neill's *The Emperor Jones*. For while the art theatres were producing avant-garde works by native playwrights, the commercial theatre, when it risked an experimental play in the early years of the decade, merely adapted foreign hits. Among these, in addition to *Beggar on Horseback*, were Luigi Pirandello's *Six Characters in Search of an Author* (1922), the Čapek brothers' *The Insect Comedy* (given under the title of *The World We Live In* [1922]), Carl

Meinhard and Rudolf Bernauer's *Johannes Kreisler* (1922), and the Harvard Dramatic Club guest production of Leonid Andreyev's *The Life of Man* (1923). This trend affected even Eva Le Gallienne's Civic Repertory Theatre, which staged Max Mohr's mildly expressionist *Improvisations in June* (*Improvisationen im Juni*) in 1928. The Mohr comedy had reputedly run two thousand nights on the Continent. The only serious experimentation on Broadway was limited to scenic design.

The earliest notable use of expressionist scenery on Broadway dates from 1921, when Robert Edmond Jones designed the settings for Arthur Hopkins's production of *Macbeth*. Jones, who had studied with Max Reinhardt in Berlin and later wrote (in *The Dramatic Imagination*) about a "new kind of drama" that would "express the activity of the subconscious mind," successfully objectified the atmosphere of *Macbeth* by means of distorted and highly stylized sets. In the words of a contemporary historian of the American theatre, "Irregular screens at one side of the stage, pierced by pointed arches, connoted not so much [Macbeth's] castle as the mood of minds distorted by murderous ambitions. Their placement at increasingly toppling angles in succeeding scenes suggested the intensifying of this mood. The leaning, unsymmetrical shapes behind the throne, and the candlesticks askew on the banquet-tables seemed to imply the crumbling of Macbeth's power." [1]

Jones's most startling innovation was the use of masks. Not only were the witches masked, but three gigantic silver masks towered over the cauldron scenes, thus visualizing what Kenneth Macgowan in his *Theatre Arts* review (April 1921) called the dominant element of *Macbeth*, "the abnormal influence of the powers symbolized by Shakespeare in the witches." The Jones-Hopkins *Macbeth* failed—perhaps because Hopkins's static direction and Lionel Barrymore's plodding acting, which bothered some critics, clashed with Jones's dynamic and imaginative sets—and Jones, though he continued to work for Hopkins, became affiliated with the Provincetown Players.

The other major scenic experiment on Broadway early in the decade, Meinhard and Bernauer's *Johannes Kreisler* (1922; MS in the Library of Congress), created quite a stir with its cleverly contrived staging effects. The play required forty-one scene changes to tell the story of an aged composer (E. T. A. Hoffmann) who recollects his melodramatic life on the eve of his death, and several of the flashbacks are objectifications of his fears or hallucinations. The ingenious set consisted of six platform stages behind a scrim, mounted on rails, and lighted by arc lamps and mirrors while the rest of the stage was in total darkness. It was capable of nightmarish effects and merited an article in the March 1923 issue of *Scientific American*.

The authors of *Johannes Kreisler*, which in the original was called *Die wunderlichen Geschichten des Kapellmeisters Kreisler* (1922), hardly qualify as serious expressionist artists. The same can be said of Paul Apel, whose *Hans Sonnenstössers Höllenfahrt* (1911) was a success in Germany before Kaufman and Connelly transformed it into *Beggar on Horseback*. Though Connelly at first denied that he or Kaufman had read the German play before writing *Beggar*, he now admits that they did read it and that they found Apel's technique more interesting than his plot, whereupon Winthrop Ames, who first told them about the play, suggested that he and Kaufman create "an American story using [Apel's] method of dreamlike association." [2]

Set in a frame of realistic action, most of *Beggar on Horseback*, which Macgowan called "the *Roger Bloomer* of the Algonquin" (*Theatre Arts*, April 1924), is the dramatization of Neil McRae's dream. The struggling composer has proposed to Gladys, the daughter of a *nouveau riche* businessman. In the dream Neil envisions his life as the son-in-law of the Cadys. The first sequence is a jazz wedding. It is set in a railway station, as if to suggest that Neil, who proposed to Gladys on the rebound, is being railroaded into matrimony. The bride carries "a bouquet that consists entirely of banknotes," [3] and most of the other exaggerations involve matters that annoyed Neil or were discussed in the previous scene. As the tempo of the dream increases, two butlers with imaginary trays multiply into a dozen automatons.

The dream turns into a nightmare when Mr. Cady takes Neil to the office and introduces him to the "widgets" business. Neil's attempt to get a pencil is presented as a hilarious spoof of the bureaucratic procedure of requisitioning. Then follows a director's meeting with the executives walking into the conference room "stiffly, in a line, repeating the phrases 'Overhead,' 'Turnover,' 'Annual Report,'. . ." (p. 135). In the restaurant scene the circling waiters move faster and faster, in time to the constantly accelerating music. When Gladys tears up the manuscript of Neil's symphony, the harassed composer murders the entire Cady family with a paper knife that is "about twice the size that it was when the audience last saw it" (p. 162). His trial is conducted in terms of a theatrical performance with ushers taking tickets and conducting the jury to their seats, and the main piece of evidence against him is one of his musical compositions, a charming little pantomime called "A Kiss in Xanadu." The jury finds it "No good" and "Highbrow," and Neil is sentenced to the Cady Consolidated Art Factory. There he is made to produce all kinds of cheap commercial music. "The ideas," he tells a visitor, "are brought from the inspiration department every hour on the hour." After he has turned them into music, "they are taken to the purifying department, and then to the testing and finishing rooms. They are then packed for shipment" (p. 220). Upon waking, Neil breaks off his engagement to Gladys. The beggar who could easily wish himself on horseback prefers to walk.

Within a year, *Beggar on Horseback* was made into a Hollywood motion picture by James Cruze. Cruze had directed *One Glorious Day* (1922) and *Hollywood* (1923), which showed the influence of *The Cabinet of Dr. Caligari*, and his use of expressionistic distortions in the motion picture version of *Beggar on Horseback* has been noted by historians of the American film.[4] The film version of *Beggar on Horseback* enjoyed great popularity in Europe, and the London production of the play seems to have left an impression on several English theatre-goers. In an introductory note to his *The Old Lady Says "No!"* the Irish playwright Denis Johnston points out that the "foster parents" of his play "are neither Evreinov, O'Neill nor Georg Kaiser," but a Continental satire that he attributes to Čapek and Kaufman and Connelly's *Beggar on Horseback*—"a superb piece of American expressionism that I have always admired." Another admirer of the play was John Galsworthy, in whose 1924 novel, *The White Monkey*, two characters converse about the meaning of expressionism.[5]

The success of *Beggar on Horseback* may have influenced Connelly to experiment with a mild form of objectification in his *Green Pastures* (1930). It certainly inspired—along with John Howard Lawson's *Processional* (launched by the Theatre Guild early in 1925) —other commercial playwrights to try their hand at expressionist dramaturgy. One of the first to do so was J. P. McEvoy. His revues, *The Comic Supplement* (closed out-of-town in 1925) and *Americana* (1926; new editions in 1928 and 1932), combine jazz-vaudeville elements with expressionistic distortions (both MSS in the New York Public Library Theatre Collection). The latter in particular employs masks, parodies a number of Eugene O'Neill's expressionist plays as well as Lawson's *Processional*, and, according to the critics, used dance routines reminiscent of the style of Balieff's *Chauve-Souris*, the Russian revue that graced Broadway in the 1920s. In 1926 the newly reorganized Actors' Theatre produced McEvoy's *God Loves Us*. Though the Actors' Theatre, an outgrowth of the Equity Players (which staged Lawson's *Roger Bloomer*) had recently merged with the Greenwich Village Theatre of Macgowan, Jones, and O'Neill, its choice of an uptown playhouse (the Maxine Elliott) and McEvoy's own commercial orientation place *God Loves Us* firmly in the Broadway category.

In *God Loves Us* (MS in the Library of Congress) McEvoy, like Kaufman and Connelly in *Beggar on Horseback*, satirically examines scenes from middle-class America. The protagonist and his wife no longer communicate with each other: when he comes home from work, she reads aloud recipes and journalistic advice to teenagers. The regimentation and tempo of a business office stifle all individuality: against a background of office sounds from rows of secretaries at typewriters and adding machines (shades of Elmer Rice!), an employee's submission to the system is objectified by means of the abbreviated language that he speaks into an impersonal telephone. An inane after-dinner speech at a business banquet reveals the vacuousness of Rotarianism: at the climax of a Father and Son Week "Go-Getter" luncheon, a minister, employing business methods in an effort to convert businessmen to Christianity, refers to St. Paul as a mail order salesman and Go-Getter who would be a credit to a modern advertising department. As McEvoy pointed out in an *Equity* interview (October 1926), what he was trying to do was "not to satirize the character . . . but those things which make him what he is—the forces behind which have moulded him." In other words, he wanted the audience "to see beyond, to recognize these 'behind' factors." The method McEvoy chose for unveiling the "beyond" reveals his indebtedness to the new mode.

Most of the characters in *God Loves Us* are types; their conversation is frequently abbreviated; certain scenes are to capture, according to the stage directions, a staccato rhythm similar to George Antheil's *Ballet Mechanique*; and the author suggests in his foreword that the action surrounding the protagonist's family should be played to the accompaniment of jazz and motion pictures. *God Loves Us* is clearly in the expressionist tradition, but, as Barrett H. Clark has pointed out in *Drama* (January 1927), the play "was written five years too late. If you have seen *Beggar on Horseback*, *The Adding Machine*, *Processional*, and Mr. McEvoy's own

Americana, you will find little new in *God Loves Us.*"
After an unsuccessful run of two weeks, McEvoy's play
was renamed *The Go Getter* and its unhappy ending was
rewritten to bring it into accord with Broadway tradition. It closed at the end of another week's run.

Another experimenter with expressionism on Broadway was William Gaston, whose *Damn the Tears*
opened at the Garrick Theatre on January 21, 1927. I
have not been able to consult a manuscript of this unpublished play, but the reviewers called it expressionistic, attacked it as another illegitimate offspring of Lawson's *Processional,* and pointed out that Norman Bel
Geddes's crazily leaning design for the insane asylum recalled *The Cabinet of Dr. Caligari.*

According to Percy Hammond of the *New York Herald Tribune* (January 22, 1927), *Damn the Tears* is
about Buckland Steele, a famous Harvard baseball player
who became a failure. The story, says Hammond, "is
presented from the point of view of this character, as he
looks at things distortedly and abandons himself to
melancholy hallucinations." Hammond goes on to say
that to express the state of Steele's mind, the producers
have gone to a great deal of trouble to create "odd and
protuberant settings and bizarre noises and extravagant
colorings." More specifically, "The scene indicating the
baseball game is full of grotesque marionettes—gigantic
effigies of the peanut and ginger pop venders and idiotic
puppets satirizing the cheer leaders and alumni." Brooks
Atkinson of the *Times* (January 22, 1927) noted that at
least two of the scenes have the "uncanny vividness" that
is the true property of expressionism, as expounded by
the playwright in a long broadside that came with the
program. And though Atkinson, like most critics, found
the play weak, he felt called upon to defend its expressionist form. "In a later scene," noted Atkinson in his
Sunday column (January 30, 1927), "when the dean
was telling Steele that he had failed in every examination, the darkening of the stage, the hiss and blare and
cries of many scattered voices off stage, recalling snatches

of the past—all this capitally portrayed the turbulence of Steele's already slightly unbalanced mind." And that is the sort of thing, concluded Atkinson, "expression[ism] can do brilliantly."

Atkinson's faith in the method of expressionism was vindicated with the Broadway production of Sophie Treadwell's *Machinal* (September 7, 1928). Undoubtedly suggested by the Ruth Snyder–Judd Gray case (with settings by Robert Edmond Jones and with Clark Gable in the role of the lover), *Machinal* tells the story of a sensitive Young Woman who marries her boss, fails to find satisfaction in the relationship, and murders him in order to be free.

As the title suggests, *Machinal* opens to the sounds of mindless mechanization, in this case of office machines, which "continue throughout the scene, and accompany the Young Woman's thoughts after the scene is blacked out." [6] The mechanical and abbreviated dialogue of the clerks captures the dull and gossipy atmosphere of a business office. The Boss has proposed to the Young Woman, and her telegraphic soliloquy reveals her desire to be married, which conflicts with her dread of physical contact. While she is pouring out her problems to her mother in episode 2, offstage voices that are projections of her desires and fears engage in courtship, marital squabbles, love making, and other domestic activities.

In a later episode the Young Woman and her husband sit at home reading newspaper headlines. She has meanwhile found happiness and sexual compatibility with another man, who has told her how he once killed two bandits with a bottle filled with pebbles. Now, as murderous thoughts come to her, the voice of her lover is heard, telling the familiar story about the bandits. As Elmer Rice had done in *The Adding Machine*, Miss Treadwell substitutes for the acutal killing an objectification of the turmoil in the murderer's mind; other voices join that of the lover to chant "stones—stones—stones," until *"the music,—the voices—mingle—increase"* and the Young Woman cries out in terror (p. 519).

In the trial scene the words and movements of people are "routine–mechanical" (p. 519); the episode ends with the Young Woman's confession and a burst of activity from the teletype machines. She who rode the subways and worked in an office full of adding machines, typewriters, and telephones is finally killed by yet another mechanical device–the electric chair. In the concluding scene the juxtaposed chanting of the priest and the matter-of-fact remarks of the reporters form a tense background against which the Young Woman's staccato outbursts of helplessness, terror, and desperate yearning for human contact find poignant expression. As in much of modern drama, the universe in *Machinal* is mechanistic and meaningless.

Brooks Atkinson (*New York Times*, September 16, 1928) found in "the episodic treatment of the story, the skeletonized settings," the "dull routine of office life," and the "tatters of office conversation" a strong resemblance to "the whole mad tumble of expressionistic drama." Yet for all the surface resemblance to the work of Kaiser and Elmer Rice, said Atkinson, *Machinal* "emerges as a triumph of individual distinction, gleaming with intangible beauty." Though several other commentators on the play, notably R. Dana Skinner,[7] criticized the work, many reviewers concurred with Atkinson. An editorial in the *Times* (September 16, 1928) went so far as to point out that "the only recent play which seems a worthy candidate for preservation is 'Machinal.'" "Its drama," continued the editorial, "is so detached, impersonal and abstract that it seems timeless. In a hundred years it should still be vital and vivid." *Machinal* has recently been successfully revived off-Broadway, and it attracted considerable attention in the European theatre, where it was staged, among others, by Tairov's Kamerny Theatre.

Miss Treadwell attempted another expressionist play with *For Saxophone* (copyright 1934; MS in the Library of Congress). Like *Machinal*, it involves a bored wife and is written in short, rapidly moving scenes. Its language is terse and disconnected, with offstage voices and music weaving a texture of counterpoint, and at times the action (as in the wedding scene, where the bride is shown to be suffocating) objectifies the protagonist's inner state.

Machinal was still packing the house at the Plymouth Theatre when Channing Pollock's *Mr. Moneypenny* opened at the Liberty Theatre in October 1928. Pollock's play, which its author has called his "best serious effort," [8] attacks the evils of materialism, but the glittering treatment of vice tends to overshadow the comparatively dull depiction of a life of virtue. (A character in the play refers to "a most delightfully dirty drama" as being "Expressionistic!") Among the dazzling scenes involving sex and money is a nightmarish episode in an office, where an enormous metronome sets the tempo of business activities, the chandelier is in the shape of a dollar mark, and gold flows down a chute into a safe. The clerks look alike, work "with a robot-like, mechanical motion, in perfect unison," [9] and the unrealistic dialogue is interrupted from time to time by such chants as "Millions—Billions! Billions—Millions!" (p. 32) In a scene of virtuous living a character dreams about married love, whereupon images of domestic bliss are projected on a movie screen in the manner of Yvan Goll's *Methusalem* (1922), a play about a rich industrialist. Mr. Moneypenny, alias Mammon, appears at one point as a ringmaster, cracking a whip at his victim, who is shown on a treadmill, struggling to catch floating hundred-dollar bills and becoming entangled in ticker-tape. When Pollock offered his play to a producer, he turned it down, recalls the author in a *New York Times* article (October 21, 1928), "because he thought it a little like 'Beggar on Horseback.'" After several other rejections, Pollock produced it himself, with Robert Edmond Jones as his designer.

Like most native expressionist plays on Broadway in the twenties, *Mr. Moneypenny* belongs in the genre of anticapitalist satire. In a way it is ironic that such dramas should have flourished in the commercial theatre. On the other hand, the reaction to President Coolidge's remark that "the business of the government is business" was perhaps inevitable. For expressionism provided the satirist with a ready-made form for caricature and grotesque exaggeration. As Stark Young pointed out in his *New Republic* review of *Beggar on Horseback* (March 5, 1924), "expressionism applied in the comic spirit to American life seems ideal," for it establishes a kind of jazz poetry and has the "flash and haste and hit-if-you-can" that is characteristic of much of American living. "It caricatures, reveals, delights." Even the proverbially tired businessman was human enough to laugh at a grotesquely ludicrous form of capitalism—especially if the satire was sugarcoated with a liberal dose of feminine pulchritude and sex appeal.

An entirely different mood of expressionism permeated Broadway when the Habima Theatre of Moscow arrived in New York and presented Eugene Vakhtangov's celebrated version of S. Ansky's *The Dybbuk* at the Mansfield Theatre in December 1926. Like such well-known Russian avant-garde directors as Vsevolod Meyerhold and Alexander Tairov, Vakhtangov experimented with nonrealistic stylization and created with *The Dybbuk* a grotesque dream vision not unlike that in *The Cabinet of Dr. Caligari.*

According to Brooks Atkinson in the *Times* (December 14, 1926), the production was "bold in its stylization." The actors moved about the stage "with grotesque motions, with absurd attitudes; the lines of the human figure [were] broken up by stooping or leaning heavily to one side." Their faces were painted to look "not unlike grotesque masks," and their voices were "individually unnatural, stressed and strained." All the benches and chairs were "off centre," and "the angular treatment" of the properties extended to the scenery, which included "oddly painted canvas, geometrical designs flung across the wings and rudely proportioned altars."

In addition to *The Dybbuk*, the Habima's New York

repertoire, all of which was characterized by grotesque distortions, consisted of David Pinski's *The Eternal Jew*, Richard Beer-Hoffman's *Jacob's Dream*, Henning Berger's *Deluge*, and Halper Leivick's *The Golem*. The latter had been given exposure as a semiexpressionist film, directed by Paul Wegener and released in this country in 1921. The visit of the Habima, which back home competed with the Moscow State Jewish Theatre (whose expressionist productions were to excite Paul Green), not only enchanted American reviewers but gave new direction to several of New York's Yiddish theatres.

Though the Yiddish Art Theatre under the direction of Maurice Schwartz had given such works as Andreyev's *Anathema* (1923) and Ernst Toller's *Hinkemann* (1924; translated as *Bloody Laughter*), the tenor of its productions had been realistic. Barely a month before the arrival of the Habima, however, the Yiddish Art Theatre staged Abraham Goldfadden's *The Tenth Commandment*. It was designed and costumed by Boris Aronson, who had come in contact with Tairov's Kamerny Theatre. As a writer in the *Theatre Arts* observed (January 1927), the production was characterized by "an intensification more common to Berlin than Broadway." The impact of the Habima itself can easily be seen in the 1928 Yiddish Art Theatre version of Jacob Gordin's *God, Man and the Devil*.

The Habima influence was even more pronounced on the Artef (*Arbeiter Theater Verband*) Players, who were organized in 1927 and whose role in the development of the American left-wing theatre of the 1930s cannot be discussed here. Suffice it to say that its director Benno Schneider was a disciple of Vakhtangov. The first work staged by Artef, B. Steinman's *At the Gate*, was called in a retrospective *New York Post* article (October 7, 1939) "an expressionistic drama"; published photographs of one of the subsequent Artef productions, Sholom Aleichem's *Aristocrats*, reveal expressionistically distorted settings. To quote a historian of the American Yiddish theatre, " 'clever and competent imitations of continental naturalism and expressionism' had been the stock-in-trade of the Yiddish theatre, reaching its high point in the production of *The Dybbuk*, and were to be brought to intensified artistic stylization in Benno Schneider's productions for the Artef group." [10]

Vakhtangov's *Dybbuk* easily transcended the language barrier (the Habima performances were in Hebrew) and enriched the theatrical culture of the lands the group visited. Though the Habima did not leave a readily discernible imprint on the work of American playwrights and directors of the late 1920s (who were following lines of similar yet independent development already charted), the type of theatre Vakhtangov—and the expressionists in general—propagated has nevertheless been slowly evolving into what has come to be called the new theatre of the 1960s. For as Brooks Atkinson noted in discussing the Habima *Dybbuk* in his Sunday column of the *Times* (December 26, 1926), the troupe had "developed a dramatic art that transcends literature in every respect and emerges as the essence of 'theatre.'" By "theatre," said Atkinson, he meant such works as O'Neill's *The Emperor Jones, The Hairy Ape*, and especially *The Great God Brown*, "a play that can have no life apart from the theatre."

Another perceptive critic who understood the potential of expressionist theatre was the *New Republic*'s Stark Young. He called the Habima *Dybbuk* the first instance of extreme stylization that he had ever seen "in which the whole of it seems inevitable" (January 5, 1927). And as if picking up Atkinson's comments, Young pursued the idea of "theatre" to its origin as ritual:

> It seems almost inevitable that we should say that the performance of The Dybbuk by the Habima Theatre of Moscow cannot be thought of as theatre: that it is religious ritual and these people priests and priestesses. Such intensity and such absorbtion might seem to belong to a sect or to the religious passion of a race.

. . . But nothing could be more mistaken. To say so is to be blind to the essence of the theatre as an art.

Expressionist theatre, whether it be a *Great God Brown* or a *Dybbuk,* has resurrected some of that ancient art and, as we will see in the next chapter, has helped to usher in the ritualistic, visually oriented theatre of the 1960s.

9

The Legacy of Expressionism

As this brief survey of a decade of experimental American drama suggests, the chauvinistic Theatre Creative had more than enough cause to take a militant, though utterly futile, stand against "the creative inspiration and intellectual stimulus from the dramatists of Europe." For Berlin-centered expressionism was as much a part of the American avant-garde theatre and drama of the 1920s as the Paris-oriented theatre of the absurd has been in the 1960s.

The affinity between expressionism and the theatre of the absurd extends beyond this superficial parallel. For a number of the American plays discussed in this study anticipate techniques or incidents in the plays of the absurd. Michael Gold's *Hoboken Blues*, for example, demands an all-Negro cast, and Gold specifies in his stage directions that the white roles are to be played by Negroes in white masks. Jean Genet later made use of the same technique in *The Blacks*. John Howard Lawson's *The International* contains a grotesque brothel scene with masked prostitutes. Outside the house of illusion revolutionaries are setting up machine guns, thus foreshadowing Genet's development of a similar situation in *The Balcony*.[1] Anticipations of the absurdists' parody of verbal clichés (as in Eugène Ionesco's *The Bald Soprano*) are to be found in Lawson's *Roger Bloomer* as well as in Elmer Rice's expressionist plays. Eugene O'Neill's *The Great God Brown* may have served Edward Albee as a model for his *Tiny Alice,* and Martin Esslin is correct in suggesting that the expressionists' subjective approach "exactly anticipates the tendency of the Theatre of the Absurd to express psychological states by objectifying them on the stage." [2] Well-known examples would be Samuel Beckett's *Waiting for Godot* and Ionesco's *Rhinoceros.*

Expressionism is clearly one of the formal ingredients of the theatre of the absurd as well as of Antonin Artaud's theatre of cruelty. Artaud, who is known to have worked with Yvan Goll and to have admired *The Cabinet of Dr. Caligari,* conceived of the essential theatre, which he likened to the plague, as an "exteriorization" of latent states. And, like Ernst Toller, who advocated skinning the human being in order to find his soul under the skin, Artaud proclaimed that "it is through the skin that metaphysics must be made to re-enter our minds." [3] Expressionism has also left a permanent impression on modern American drama from its birth in the teens of our century to the current off-off-Broadway movement. Though there was never an expressionist movement as such in the United States, most significant American playwrights have availed themselves of certain aspects of expressionistic dramaturgy.

In the 1930s expressionist elements enlivened the matter-of-fact content of the crude left-wing agitprop plays, and social revolutionaries argued on the pages of *Workers' Theatre* (later renamed *New Theatre*) whether to use realism or expressionism in order to undermine the bourgeois theatre. One of the most successful productions of the League of Workers' Theatre (later the New Theatre League) was Irwin Shaw's *Bury the Dead* (1936). This work invites comparison with Ernst Toller's *Transformation* as well as with another experimental Continental drama, Hans Chlumberg's *Miracle at Verdun* (*Wunder um Verdun*), which the Theatre Guild staged in 1931.

Another workers' stage group of the thirties was the Theatre Union. It opened its first season in November

1933 with *Peace on Earth* by George Sklar and Albert Maltz. This antiwar play begins realistically but ends with an expressionistic dream sequence. In talking with the present writer, both Sklar and Maltz reminisced about such possible influences as Henri-René Lenormand's *Failures* (staged by the Guild in 1923), the plays of German expressionism, the work of the New Playwrights, Sophie Treadwell's *Machinal*, and Professor George Pierce Baker's Yale productions of Velona Pilcher's *The Searcher* (published 1929) and Harold Igo's *Steel* (1930).[4] Igo's *Steel* (MS in the Library of Congress) is strongly reminiscent of O'Neill's *The Hairy Ape* and *Dynamo*. Velona Pilcher's *The Searcher* borrows its subject matter and technique from several Continental plays.

Expressionist elements can also be found in the work of the Federal Theatre Project, which was headed by Hallie Flanagan, a former student of Professor Baker's and for a decade the director of the Vassar Experimental Theatre. Mrs. Flanagan encountered European expressionism at first hand while traveling abroad, and at Vassar she produced Toller, agitprops, an expressionist version of Chekhov's *The Marriage Proposal*, as well as the world première of T. S. Eliot's contribution to expressionism, *Sweeney Agonistes*. Under Mrs. Flanagan's direction, the Federal Theatre gave plays by O'Neill, Rice, Lawson, and Alfred Kreymborg. Of the many new plays that it produced, John Hunter Booth's *Created Equal* (MS in the Library of Congress) serves as an example of the expressionist social protest play of the thirties. The work makes use of masks and contains a scene with a huge stock ticker that emits enormous quantities of ribbon. Top-hatted plutocrats, chewing fat cigars, study the tape while voices in the background speak in disconnected language. The Federal Theatre also made plans to stage *The Dog beneath the Skin* by W. H. Auden and Christopher Isherwood, which, like the other 1930s collaborations of these two Anglo-Americans, contains characteristically expressionistic episodes.

The most original contribution of the Federal Theatre was the Living Newspaper, which dramatized current social and economic problems by means of a variety of techniques, including choral chants, stylized action, and the use of loudspeakers and projections. Influenced by the work of the Soviet Blue Blouse troupes as well as by Brecht and Piscator, the Living Newspapers frequently distort character, speech, setting, time, and action in order to express inner meanings. Thus in *Power* (1937) the justices of the Supreme Court, hearing arguments on the TVA case, are represented by nine forbidding masks placed on a high bench. In *1935* (1936) Louisiana legislators are depicted as lifeless puppets whose strings are literally pulled by Huey Long. And when Arthur Arent's *One-Third of a Nation* (1938) was initially staged at a Vassar workshop, the set designer endeavored to arouse the emotions of the audience by enlarging or distorting common household items, such as a faucet, a garbage can, a toilet seat, in order to convey to the spectator the feeling of how "life in slum conditions distorts such objects." [5]

Traces of expressionism are to be found, furthermore, in the plays of Archibald MacLeish, and recent scholarship has paid increasing attention to the same mode in the work of Thornton Wilder. In a 1948 address at the University of Frankfort, Wilder acknowledged his debt to German expressionism, and in a 1951 letter, he wrote, "Way back in 1920 and 1921 I read all the Kokoschka plays I could find; I collected them in Rome through a bookstore." [6]

In the 1940s expressionism left its mark on the plays of William Saroyan and William Carlos Williams and invaded the field of musical comedy with such works as Rodgers and Hammerstein's *Allegro* (1947) and Kurt Weill and Moss Hart's *Lady in the Dark* (1941). In the Hart musical, Liza Elliott's Freudian dreams are acted out with the help of grotesquely distorted properties, and at one point Liza's lover appears as a circus ringmaster, snapping a whip in the manner of Mr. Moneypenny in

Channing Pollock's play. The circus scene then changes into a courtroom, reminiscent of the musical dream-trial in *Beggar on Horseback*. In his autobiography, Hart has written about the impact this Kaufman and Connelly comedy made on him. Another important influence on Hart was a young man who talked of Vsevolod Meyerhold and Georg Kaiser.[7]

The shadows of Meyerhold and Kaiser loom even larger over the work of many post–World War II American playwrights from Arthur Laurents (*A Clearing in the Woods*) to Adrienne Kennedy (*The Owl Answers*) and Tom Eyen (*The White Whore and the Bit Player*). And the plays of the three universally recognized American dramatists of this period—Arthur Miller, Tennessee Williams, and Edward Albee—are all indebted to expressionist dramaturgy.

Seven years after the production of his semiexpressionistic *Death of a Salesman* (1949), Miller pondered the question of dramatic form in an essay published in the April 1956 issue of the *Atlantic Monthly*, where he suggests that there are two general ideas that govern the choosing of the right form. These are the ideas of family and society. The first demands realism, while social relationships are best revealed through expressionism. In defining expressionism, Miller cites among other examples O'Neill's *The Great God Brown* and Kaiser's *Gas*. He then analyzes Wilder's *Our Town* as an example of social expressionism. In the light of his own subsequent development toward what might be considered to be an epic dramaturgy in *After the Fall* (1964), it is significant that Miller should have focused on *Our Town*, a play which is consciously didactic, utilizes the device of the narrator, and contains other epic alienation effects. Like Brecht and Lawson before him, Miller has moved from expressionism to epic theatre.

In the introduction to his *Collected Plays*, Miller states that he "had always been attracted and repelled by the brilliance of German expressionism."[8] A less ambiguous view is held by Tennessee Williams. "Expressionism and all other unconventional techniques in drama," writes Williams in the production notes to *The Glass Menagerie* (1945), "have only one valid aim, and that is a closer approach to truth. . . . Everyone should know nowadays the unimportance of the photographic in art: that truth, life, or reality is an organic thing which the poetic imagination can represent or suggest, in essence, only through transformation, through changing into other forms than those which were merely present in appearance." [9] These "other forms" appear here and there in Williams's plays (e.g., the objectification of the terror in Blanche's mind in *A Streetcar Named Desire* [1947] by means of grotesquely distorted visual and aural images) and find their most sustained application in *Camino Real* (1953). Its street cleaners probably derive from John Dos Passos's *The Garbage Man*, and its debt to Continental experiments has been summed up by George Jean Nathan (*Theatre Arts*, June 1953), who called *Camino Real* "a cold stew of Kaiser expressionism, Cocteau extravaganza, Wedekind sexual anarchy, Strindberg nightmare fancy, Stein aural theory, Sartre dead-end philosophy, and Schönberg tonal technic."

Edward Albee, whose *The American Dream* (1961) contains numerous distortions, has called his *Tiny Alice* (1964) "a metaphysical dream play which must be entered into and experienced without predetermination of how a play is supposed to go." [10] By calling it "a metaphysical dream play," Albee has placed his own work in the tradition of dramatic expressionism that goes back to Strindberg's dream plays. Thus we are justified in approaching *Tiny Alice* as an objectification of Brother Julian's nightmare or hallucination.

Albee's *Tiny Alice* not only contains a number of familiar expressionist techniques (masks, visually expressed transferals of personality, symbolic distortions of reality), but derives in part from O'Neill's *The Great God Brown*.[11] Other plays of the 1960s are indebted to American expressionist plays of earlier decades, primarily of the 1920s. For example, Frank Gagliano's *Father Ux-*

bridge Wants to Marry (1967) and the *Interview* part of Jean-Claude Van Itallie's *America Hurrah* (1966) owe something to Rice's *The Adding Machine*. Murray Schisgal's *The Typists* (1963) borrows nonrealistic techniques from both *The Adding Machine* and Wilder's *The Long Christmas Dinner*. Lewis John Carlino's *Objective Case* (1963) is reminiscent of Edmund Wilson's *Cronkhite's Clocks*. Lanford Wilson's *Wandering* (1966) brings to mind Alfred Kreymborg's *Manikin and Minikin*. The grotesque puppets and masks of the *Motel* part of *America Hurrah* (or, for that matter, of the Bread and Puppet Theatre), while probably indebted to the theories of Gordon Craig, are not unlike the giant effigies of cheerleaders and pop venders in William Gaston's *Damn the Tears*. The curtain scene of act 2, scene 2, of James Paul Dey's *Passacaglia* (copyright 1968) is strongly evocative of the murder sequence in *The Adding Machine*, as is a section of Red Grooms's 1959 Happening *The Burning Building*, whose sets bring to mind *The Cabinet of Dr. Caligari*. The list is endless.

Similarly, the new centers of avant-garde drama, such as the Caffe Cino, Café La Mama (later La Mama E.T.C.–Experimental Theatre Club), the Living Theatre, the Judson Poets' Theatre, Theatre Genesis, and the Open Theatre, are the spiritual heirs of the Provincetown Players, the Washington Square Players, the Neighborhood Playhouse, and the New Playwrights' Theatre. What is, however, considerably more significant than these parallels suggest, involves the much-delayed transposition of the Continental expressionist *Weltanschauung* to the current American scene. The contemporary underground culture has not only given birth to a group of dynamic off-off-Broadway theatres, but its world view of passion and pacifism, morbidity and mysticism, brotherhood and primitivism, irrationality and anarchism, hallucinatory states of mind and anti-Establishment attitudes is strongly reminiscent of the spirit of *Menschheitsdämmerung* that on the one hand despaired of bourgeois philistinism, family restraints, militarism, machine civilization, and the bureaucracy of the Weimar Republic, and on the other hand cried *O Mensch!* in anticipation of the New Man.

The extent of the indebtedness of the visually oriented new American drama of the sixties to expressionistic dramaturgy (as well as to other movements influenced by expressionism, such as the art film and the theatre of the absurd) is suggested by the director's notes to Megan Terry's *Keep Tightly Closed in a Cool Dry Place*. The play, says its author, "can be directed literally or as a fantasy or dream," and its three characters can be seen "as aspects of one personality." In talking about the Open Theatre production of *Keep Tightly Closed*, the director states that the formal innovations of Miss Terry's play have been anticipated by earlier forms of theatre, including "Expressionistic plays such as Sorge's *The Beggar*," the films of Federico Fellini, and the work of the absurdist playwrights, who (like Toller, O'Neill, and Artaud) attempt to get "beyond the nervous system into the soul." [12]

Most serious playwrights since the 1920s have grasped the imaginative tools of expressionist dramaturgy in order to hack through what O'Neill called "the banality of surfaces." Numerically, the expressionistic twenties in American drama did not produce many plays. It is significant, however, that our leading playwrights from O'Neill to Albee and beyond have made use of such expressionistic techniques of objective distortion as grotesque visual imagery, symbolic action, heightened language, exaggerated characters, and rapidly shifting scenes. The subject matter of Continental expressionism survived the transatlantic journey less well, though there is a strong social awareness, coupled with a negative attitude toward mechanization, in O'Neill, Rice, Sophie Treadwell, Edmund Wilson, and Lawson, as well as the other members of the New Playwrights' Theatre. Even the New Man makes an occasional appearance in the work of some American playwrights (e.g., Lawson, Dos

Passos), and there is a comic echo of the somber Teutonic battle of the generations (see Arnolt Bronnen's *Parricide* [*Vatermord*, 1922]) in *The Adding Machine*, where a character tells how he raised his knife to carve a leg of lamb but instead cut his mother's throat. Thus the spirit of many American expressionist plays of the twenties is much lighter and more playfully satiric than that of German expressionism.

At the same time, it must be kept in mind that of all the expressionist playwrights it is the American Eugene O'Neill who has gained the widest international recognition. O'Neill may not always have thought like an expressionist, but he certainly wrote like one between 1920 and 1934. As a consequence, the meaning of a play like *The Great God Brown* is frequently to be sought in its form. For example, the mask that Margaret embraces in the concluding scene of that play dramatically reveals a wife's failure to understand her husband even in death. Thus much of the credit for the current shift of dramaturgy from the verbal to the visual must go to expressionist playwrights.

In a front-page article in the *New York Herald Tribune* drama section for September 23, 1928, Richard Watts, Jr., who had reported from these pages for a number of years, attempted a brief critical overview of American expressionism. According to Watts, expressionism "gave evidence of being the most invigorating force in the American drama" with such plays as Lawson's *Processional*, Rice's *The Adding Machine*, John Dos Passos's *The Moon is a Gong* (i.e., *The Garbage Man*) and Edmund Wilson's *The Crime in the Whistler Room*. Then "the period of decadence arrived" with the work of the New Playwrights' Theatre and Cummings's *Him*. Now, however, says Watts, "expressionism [has] . . . provided the best play of the new season" with Sophie Treadwell's *Machinal*. For *Machinal* "proves pretty definitely that expressionism is not necessarily the work of a faddist or one too unskilled to limit herself to the austere confines of the well-made play."

Watts's pronouncements are typical of the views of many of the critics of the twenties concerning the American expressionist drama of that decade. O'Neill and other early experimenters with the form, such as Alfred Kreymborg and Susan Glaspell, are pretty much ignored. This is perhaps understandable in the case of Kreymborg and Glaspell, whose work at the tiny Provincetown Playhouse escaped the attention of most theatregoers. The neglect of O'Neill is more surprising, for his fame soon transcended the narrow confines of the Provincetown stage. But as the editors of a recent volume on O'Neill point out, his critics "for the most part remained loyal to naturalism and hardly noticed his attempts to bring new forms to the American stage." The same scholars find it significant that the word *expressionism* or *expressionistic* does not appear in the reviews of *The Emperor Jones, The Hairy Ape, All God's Chillun Got Wings*, and *The Great God Brown* that they assembled for inclusion in their volume.[13]

Though Watts's views represent the conventional attitude, the reality, as this study has endeavored to show, is quite different. For the application of expressionist techniques—the use of distortion to present subjective states—was much more widespread than Watts's summary indicates. Hence a more accurate periodization of American expressionist drama of the 1920s would divide the decade into four phases. The first stirrings of the new mode extend back to the experiments of Theodore Dreiser and Alfred Kreymborg in 1916. This exploratory period comes to an end with the 1921 Provincetown Playhouse production of Susan Glaspell's *The Verge*. Included in this phase are the early plays of Eugene O'Neill. With the Provincetown production of O'Neill's *The Hairy Ape* (and the Theatre Guild's staging of Georg Kaiser's *From Morn to Midnight*) in the spring of 1922, the term *expressionism* gains wide currency, and the first flowering of American expressionist drama, lasting until 1926, begins. Among the major works of this period are, in addition to *The Hairy Ape*,

Elmer Rice's *The Adding Machine,* John Howard Lawson's *Processional,* Kaufman and Connelly's *Beggar on Horseback,* and O'Neill's *The Great God Brown.* This is also the time when the Provincetown Players stage a number of European as well as native expressionist plays. The third period, 1926–28, is characterized by increasing social activism as well as commercialization of expressionist plays, which dominate the boards of the New Playwrights' Theatre and lose their novelty even on Broadway. As if in reaction to the mediocrity of the plays of this period, the final phase, 1928–29, which includes O'Neill's association with the Theatre Guild, launches such important works as Sophie Treadwell's *Machinal* and E. E. Cummings's *Him.*

Watts must be corrected, furthermore, in his critical opinions. For the most aesthetically satisfying American expressionist plays of the twenties are the ones he disliked or neglected to mention at all—Cummings's *Him* and O'Neill's *The Great God Brown.* Running close behind these two in dramatic effectiveness are O'Neill's *The Emperor Jones* and *The Hairy Ape,* to be followed by Kreymborg's *Vote the New Moon,* Paul Green's *Tread the Green Grass,* Dos Passos's *The Garbage Man,* Kaufman and Connelly's *Beggar on Horseback,* Treadwell's *Machinal,* Lawson's *Processional,* and Rice's *The Adding Machine* (though *The Subway* is a more sustained expressionist work than *The Adding Machine,* just as Lawson's *Roger Bloomer* is stylistically purer than his *Processional*).

Discussing *Processional,* Joseph Wood Krutch has observed that expressionism "seemed capable of expressing as no other method could the confused emotions of that section of the intellectual public which agreed with Mr. Aldous Huxley when he said: 'The mind has lost its Aristotelian elegance of shape.'" Or, as Ezra Pound wrote in 1920 [14]

> *The age demanded an image*
> *Of its accelerated grimace,*

Something for the modern stage,
Not, at any rate, an Attic grace.

By dramatizing the inner life of twentieth-century man, whose mind reaches beyond Aristotelian refinement and Attic grace toward the terrors of his collective unconscious, American expressionism of the 1920s has added to the modern repertoire a significant body of vivid and dynamic plays that reflect the accelerated grimace of our age.

Notes

1 – The Spell of Expressionism

1. "Theatre Creative Is All-American," *New York Times*, September 20, 1926, p. 21. "Creative But Native," *New York Times* editorial, September 21, 1926, p. 28.

2. Albert Soergel, *Dichtung und Dichter der Zeit. Neue Folge: Im Banne des Expressionismus*, 4th ed. (Leipzig, 1927), p. 357. For the best introduction to German expressionism and its worldwide ramifications (as well as a useful bibliography) see John Willett, *Expressionism* (New York, 1970).

3. Trans. Michael Sadleir et al. (New York, 1947), p. 75.

4. Kasimir Edschmid, "Über den dichterischen Expressionismus," reprinted in Edschmid, *Frühe Manifeste: Epochen des Expressionismus* (Hamburg, 1957), pp. 33, 34. "Die Tatsachen haben Bedeutung nur so weit, als, durch sie hindurchgreifend, die Hand des Künstlers nach dem fasst, was hinter ihnen steht. . . . Die Welt ist da. Es wäre sinnlos, sie zu wiederholen. Sie im letzten Zucken, im eigentlichsten Kern aufzusuchen und neu zu schaffen, das ist die grösste Aufgabe der Kunst." "Über die dichterische deutsche Jugend," in Edschmid, *Frühe Manifeste*, p. 18. "Der Weg der Dichtung unserer Tage führt aus der Hülle zur Seele, aus dem Rang zum Menschen, von Schildern zum Geist." The *Sturm* definition of expressionism is quoted in Soergel, p. 589. "Expressionismus 'ist die geistige Bewegung einer Zeit, die das innere Erlebnis über das äussere Leben stellt.' " My translations.

5. *The Writer in Extremis: Expressionism in Twentieth-Century German Literature* (Stanford, Calif., 1959), pp. 61–62.

6. Carl Dahlström, *Strindberg's Dramatic Expressionism*, 2nd ed. (New York, 1968), p. 61.

7. In August Strindberg, *Eight Expressionist Plays*, trans. Arvid Paulson (New York, 1965), p. 343.

8. "Expressionism," trans. Joseph Bernstein, in *Actors on Acting*, ed. Toby Cole and Helen Krich Chinoy (New York, 1949), pp. 279–80. Reprinted as "Epilogue to the Actor," in *Anthology of German Expressionist Drama*, ed. Walter H. Sokel (Garden City, N.Y., 1963), pp. 7–8.

9. "My Works," trans. Marketa Goetz, *Tulane Drama Review*, 3 (March 1959), 100. The expressionists' concern with abbreviated language was anticipated by Swift's professors of the Grand Academy of Lagado, whom Gulliver encounters during his third voyage: "The first project was to shorten discourse by cutting polysyllables into one, and leaving out verbs and participles, because in reality all things imaginable are but nouns."

10. *World Drama: From Aeschylus to Anouilh* (New York, n.d.), p. 810.

2 – The Provincetown Players: Jig Cook

1. Arthur and Barbara Gelb, *O'Neill* (New York, 1962), pp. 270–71. Cf. Susan Glaspell, *The Road to the Temple* (New York, 1927), p. 248.

2. Quoted in Kenneth Macgowan, *Footlights Across America* (New York, 1929), p. 7.

3. Helen Deutsch and Stella Hanau, *The Provincetown* (New York, 1931), pp. 11, 23, 15.

4. Quoted in Alfred Kreymborg, *Troubadour* (New York, 1925), p. 305. See also the introduction to Kreymborg, ed., *Poetic Drama* (New York, 1941), p. 39.

5. Kreymborg, *Plays for Poem-Mimes* (New York, 1918), pp. 29, 30. Subsequent references to this volume will appear in the text.

6. Kreymborg, *Plays for Merry Andrews* (New York, 1920), p. 14.

7. Kreymborg, *Troubadour*, p. 162.

8. Moody E. Prior, *The Language of Tragedy* (New York, 1947), p. 376. Waldo Frank, "Mr. Kreymborg Woos America," *Dial*, 79 (July 1925), 72.

9. Quoted in Richard Dana Skinner, *Eugene O'Neill: A Poet's Quest* (New York, 1935), p. viii.

10. *The Plays of Eugene O'Neill*, 3 vols. (New York, 1955), 1: 489. Quotations from O'Neill's plays are from this standard edition. Volume and page references will appear in the text.

11. Quoted in Agnes Boulton, *Part of a Long Story* (Garden City, N.Y., 1958), p. 242.

12. Boston, 1922, p. 58. Subsequent references will appear in the text.

3 – Eugene O'Neill

1. *Brecht on Theatre*, ed. and trans. John Willett (New York, 1964), p. 68. O'Neill's denial is quoted in Barrett H. Clark, *Eugene O'Neill: The Man and His Plays*, rev. ed. (New York, 1947), p. 83. See also Malcolm Cowley, "A Weekend with Eugene O'Neill," *Reporter*, 17 (September 5, 1957), 35; reprinted in *O'Neill and His Plays: Four Decades of Criticism*, ed. Oscar Cargill et al. (New York, 1961), p. 46.

2. Quoted in Wisner Payne Kinne, *George Pierce Baker and the American Theatre* (Cambridge, Mass., 1954), p. 184.

3. Clark, p. 25. Cf. O'Neill to Beatrice Ashe Maher, September 10, 1914 and November 8, 1914, MSS in the Berg Collection, New York Public Library.

4. *Revolt in German Drama* (Girard, Kansas, "Little Blue Book").

5. Interview with Mary Heaton Vorse, Provincetown, Mass., August 3, 1963.

6. In Isaac Goldberg, *The Theatre of George Jean Nathan* (New York, 1926), p. 149. Reprinted in Cargill, p. 101.

7. Agnes Boulton, "An Experimental Theatre: The Provincetown Playhouse," *Theatre Arts*, 8 (March 1924), 185.

8. *The Plays of Eugene O'Neill*, 3 vols. (New York, 1955), 3:189. Subsequent references to the plays in this volume will appear in the text.

9. For the reception of *The Emperor Jones* in Germany see Horst Frenz, "Eugene O'Neill on the German Stage," *Theatre Annual*, 11 (1953), 27–29. Emmel's book, *Das ekstatische Theater*, was published in Prien in 1924. "Hier

ist Bühnenatem. Dramatische Kraft. Tragische Verwurzelung. . . . Endlich ein Drama" (p. 320). My translation.

10. Quoted in Arthur and Barbara Gelb, *O'Neill* (New York, 1962), p. 492.

11. Gelb and Gelb, p. 495.

12. Trans. Winifred Katzin (New York, 1963), pp. 39–40. Some of these parallels have been noted by Clara Blackburn, "Continental Influences on Eugene O'Neill's Expressionistic Dramas," *American Literature*, 13(1941), 118–20. See also Edwin A. Engel, *The Haunted Heroes of Eugene O'Neill* (Cambridge, Mass., 1953), p. 55.

13. *O'Neill* (Edinburgh, 1963), p. 37.

14. O'Neill to Ralph Block, June 10, 1921, MS courtesy of The Walter Hampden Memorial Library at the Players, New York. Cf. O'Neill's letter to Theresa Helburn (n.d.), in Helburn, *A Wayward Quest* (Boston, 1960), p. 277. According to a notation which concludes the MS of *The Hairy Ape* (Princeton University Library), the play was begun on December 7 and finished on December 23, 1921. For the short story see O'Neill's letter to Richard Dana Skinner, in Skinner, *Eugene O'Neill: A Poet's Quest* (New York, 1935), p. viii.

15. See Cleon Throckmorton, "Overshooting the Mark," *Little Review*, 11 (Winter 1926), 97.

16. Mardi Valgemae, "Eugene O'Neill's Preface to *The Great God Brown*," *Yale University Library Gazette*, 43 (July 1968), 29.

17. July 6, 1925, holograph draft of telegram in the Dartmouth College Library Landauer Collection. See also León Mirlas's interpretation of *The Great God Brown* and O'Neill's letter to this South American critic in *O'Neill y el teatro contemporáneo*, by León Mirlas, 2nd ed. (Buenos Aires, 1961), p. 203.

18. Yvan Goll, "Two Superdramas," trans. Walter H. Sokel, in *Anthology of German Expressionist Drama*, ed. Walter Sokel (Garden City, N.Y., 1963), p. 10. Lothar Schreyer, *Expressionistisches Theater* (Hamburg, 1948), pp. 218–19. "Maske ist die äussere Hülle des Menschen, sie hüllt nicht nur das Gesicht ein, sondern den ganzen Körper und die ganze Wesenheit des Menschen. Persona ist das Wort von gleicher Bedeutung. . . . So ist die Maske des Bühnenwerkes eine gedichtete Ausstrahlung der Idee des

Wesens, eine Ausstrahlung, die in Form und Farbe die Idee verkündet." My translation. Edward Gordon Craig, "The Artist of the Future," *The Mask*, 1 (May–June 1908), 58.

19. Erik Reger, "Der Georg Kaiser von Amerika," *Die Literatur*, 31 (1928–29), 272. The best recent examination of O'Neill's experimental dramaturgy is Egil Törnqvist's *A Drama of Souls: Studies in O'Neill's Super-Naturalistic Technique* (New Haven, Conn., 1969). See also Timo Tiusanen, *O'Neill's Scenic Images* (Princeton, N.J., 1968).

4 – The Provincetown Players: The Triumvirate and After

1. Reprinted in *O'Neill and His Plays: Four Decades of Criticism*, ed. Oscar Cargill et al. (New York, 1961), pp. 108–9.

2. Quoted in Arthur and Barbara Gelb, *O'Neill* (New York, 1962), p. 525.

3. All references to *The Ancient Mariner* are from the text edited by Donald Gallup, *Yale University Library Gazette*, 35 (October 1960), 63–86.

4. June 2, 1930, printed in "O'Neill Says Soviet Stage Has Realized His Dream," *New York Herald Tribune*, June 19, 1932, sec. 7, p. 2. Reprinted in Cargill, p. 123.

5. Peter Fleming, "Red and Black," *Spectator*, 150 (June 30, 1933), 940. Eugene O'Neill, "Second Thoughts," *American Spectator*, 1 (December 1932), 2. Reprinted in Cargill, p. 119.

6. Sherman Paul, *Edmund Wilson* (Urbana, Ill., 1965), p. 41.

7. In Edmund Wilson, *Five Plays* (New York, 1954), p. 173. Subsequent references to this play will appear in the text.

8. See, for example. "The Rag-Bag of the Soul," *Literary Review* of the *New York Evening Post*, November 25, 1922, p. 237. See also Wilson's satiric treatment of expressionist drama in "Fire-Alarm," *New Republic*, 50 (April 20, 1927), 250–52.

9. *The Field God And In Abraham's Bosom* (New York, 1927), p. 122.

10. Typescript, p. 1–1, MS at the Egri-Cornell Writers

Workshop, New York. Subsequent references will appear in the text. The play was originally written in Hungarian.

11. In E. E. Cummings, *Three Plays and a Ballet* (New York, 1967), p. 10. Subsequent references will appear in the text.

12. *i: six nonlectures* (Cambridge, Mass., 1953), p. 82. See also Cummings's letter to Norman Friedman, in Friedman, *e. e. cummings* (Carbondale, Ill., 1964), p. 58.

13. "[Notes on] Him (1927)," *From the Modern Repertoire: Series Two* (Bloomington, Ind., 1952), p. 490.

14. *him AND the CRITICS*, n.d., p. 8 (Edmund Wilson) and p. 10 (S. Foster Damon), The New York Public Library Theatre Collection. Jaques Barzun, "E. E. Cummings: A Word About *Him*," *Harvard Wake*, no. 5 (spring 1946), 56. John Howard Lawson, *Theory and Technique of Playwriting*, rev. ed. (New York, 1960), p. 120.

15. *Expressionistisches Theater* (Hamburg, 1948), p. 161. "Das Werk ist als Dichtung und innere Schau des Theaters—imaginatives Theater!—so bedeutend, dass es die Zeitgebundenheit aller expressionistischen deutschen Wortkunstwerke für die Bühne überragt. Es könnte berufen sein, den Weg des Theaters, wie er durch die im Expressionismus gewonnenen Erkenntnisse bestimmt ist, schöpferisch weiterzuführen." My translation.

16. Paul Green, *The House of Connelly And Other Plays* (New York, 1931), p. 232. Subsequent references will appear in the text.

17. Trans. Ruth Langner (New York, 1926), p. 107.

18. Agatha Boyd Adams, *Paul Green of Chapel Hill* (Chapel Hill, N.C., 1951), pp. 44–45, 55, 68.

19. Adams, p. 43. Paul Green, *Drama and the Weather* (New York, 1958), pp. 15, 22.

5—Elmer Rice

1. *The Magic Curtain* (New York, 1951), p. 142.

2. *The Plays of Eugene O'Neill* (New York, 1955), 3, 473. Quotations from O'Neill's plays are from this edition. Volume and page references will appear in the text.

3. Quoted in Ward Morehouse, "Playwriting's Old Pro," *Theatre Arts*, 43 (April 1959), 19.

4. Quoted in Sister Ann Gertrude Coleman, "Expressionism—40 Years After," *CEA Critic*, 27 (June 1965), 1, 7. In

his *Minority Report: An Autobiography* (New York, 1963), p. 198, Rice says that he had read Strindberg and Andreyev, and he focuses attention on Theodore Dreiser's *Plays of the Natural and the Supernatural,* "which contain several remarkable expressionistic one-act plays."

5. Elmer Rice, *Minority Report,* pp. 198–99.

6. Elmer Rice, *The Living Theatre* (New York, 1959), p. 1.

7. London, 1924 (First published 1916), p. 235. Italics added. *Ulysses in Nighttown,* a dramatization of Joyce's *Ulysses,* was given a successful expressionistic production in New York in 1958.

8. New York, 1923, p. 1. Subsequent references to this play will appear in the text.

9. Elmer Rice, *Three Plays* (New York, 1965), p. 25.

10. *Minority Report,* pp. 215, 218.

11. "Apologia Pro Vita Sua, Per Elmer Rice," *New York Times,* December 25, 1938, sec. 9, p. 5. Cf. Robert Hogan, *The Independence of Elmer Rice* (Carbondale, Ill., 1965), pp. 39, 41, and Gerald Rabkin, *Drama and Commitment* (Bloomington, Ind., 1964), pp. 245–46.

12. New York, 1929, p. 20. Subsequent references will appear in the text.

13. Trans. Ashley Dukes (New York, 1922), p. 151. Haskell M. Block, "Expressionism in Modern American Drama," *Comparative Literature,* Proceedings of the Second Congress of ICLA, vol. 2 (Chapel Hill, N.C., 1959), suggests that Eugene's epic of industrialism entitled "The Subway," which ends with an apocalyptic vision of the destruction of civilization, is "strikingly reminiscent of the vision of mass annihilation" in Kaiser's *Gas I* (p. 539).

14. *Minority Report,* p. 402.

15. New York, 1940, p. 18.

16. *Minority Report,* p. 236.

17. New York, 1932, p. 56.

18. Owen Barfield, "Changes in the Theatre," *Theatre Arts Monthly,* 8 (September 1924), 641.

6—John Howard Lawson

1. "The Guild Apologizes" and "A Spirited Debate," *The Theatre Guild Bulletin,* no. 5 (February 1925), pp. 1, 2.

H. I. Brock, "American Dance of Life Rhymed to Jazz," *New York Times Magazine,* February 1, 1925, p. 18.

2. Unless otherwise documented, specific information concerning Mr. Lawson and his plays was furnished by the playwright in a series of conversations in Los Angeles, California, in the summer of 1966.

3. *The Theme is Freedom* (New York, 1956), p. 41.

4. Grace Anshutz, "Expressionistic Drama in the American Theatre," *Drama,* 16 (April 1926), 246. Ludwig Lewisohn, "Native Plays," *Nation,* 116 (March 21, 1923), 346.

5. New York, 1923, p. 5. Subsequent references will appear in the text. For an account of the two productions of *Roger Bloomer* as well as an analysis of its expressionistic elements see A. R. Fulton, "Expressionism: John Howard Lawson," in *Drama and Theatre,* ed. A. R. Fulton (New York, 1946), pp. 200–209.

6. New York, 1925, pp. v, ix. Subsequent references to the play will appear in the text. Cf. Montrose J. Moses, *The American Dramatist* (Boston, 1925), pp. 435–36.

7. O'Neill to Michael Gold, February 12, 1925; MS in the Dartmouth College Library.

8. Typescript, p. I–1, in Mr. Lawson's personal files, hereafter referred to as "Lawson papers." Subsequent references to the play will appear in the text.

9. Quoted in Stanley J. Kunitz et al., *Authors Today and Yesterday* (New York, 1933), p. 397.

10. New York, 1927, p. x. Subsequent references will appear in the text.

11. "The New Playwrights: Theatrical Insurgency in Pre-Depression America," *Theatre Survey,* 2 (1961), 42.

12. *The International* (New York, 1927), p. 8. Subsequent references to the play will appear in the text.

13. *Drama and Commitment* (Bloomington, Ind., 1964), pp. 141–42.

14. Werner Neuse, *Die literarische Entwicklung von John Dos Passos* (Giessen, 1931), p. 87.

15. Quoted in Kunitz, p. 397.

7 – The New Playwrights' Theatre

1. George A. Knox and Herbert M. Stahl, *Dos Passos and "The Revolting Playwrights"* (Upsala, 1964).

2. Unless otherwise documented, specific information concerning the New Playwrights' Theatre was furnished by Mr. Lawson in a series of conversations in Los Angeles, California, in the summer of 1966.

3. New York, 1927, p. 77.

4. New York, 1927.

5. New York, 1927, p. 9. Subsequent references will appear in the text.

6. New York, 1931, p. 154.

7. In *The American Caravan*, ed. Van Wyck Brooks, Alfred Kreymborg, et al. (New York, 1927), p. 548. Subsequent references will appear in the text.

8. Mencken to Sinclair, December 12, 1923, printed in Upton Sinclair, *My Lifetime in Letters* (Columbia, Mo., 1960), p. 237. O'Neill to Sinclair, March 26, 1923, ibid., p. 279. In a letter to the *New York Times* (December 23, 1928), Sinclair insists that "all the devices of the so-called 'constructivist' or 'expressionist' technique are found" in his play *The Pot Boiler* (Girard, Kan., 1924), which he wrote in 1913 and which was staged in Pasadena, California, in 1916, "prior to the production of any of the 'expressionist' plays in Germany." Sinclair is here overstating his claim.

9. Long Beach, Calif., 1924, p. 63.

10. O'Neill to Sinclair, August 22, 1924, in the Lilly Library of Indiana University. Zangwill to Sinclair, December 31, 1924, printed in Sinclair, *My Lifetime in Letters*, p. 313. Floyd Dell, *Upton Sinclair* (New York, 1927), pp. 179–80. For *Singing Jailbirds* in Berlin see Erwin Piscator, *Das Politische Theater* (Berlin, 1929), p. 229.

11. New York, 1926, p. 121. Subsequent references will appear in the text.

12. *Pinwheel* (New York, 1927), p. 3. Subsequent references will appear in the text.

13. June 16, 1928, printed in Knox and Stahl, p. 82.

14. *Most Likely to Succeed* (New York, 1954), p. 137.

8 – Broadway and Beyond

1. Oliver M. Sayler, *Our American Theatre* (New York, 1923), p. 211.

2. Marc Connelly, *Voices Offstage: A Book of Memoirs* (New York, 1968), p. 118. For the denial see Arthur Hob-

son Quinn, *A History of the American Drama From the Civil War to the Present Day* (New York, 1936), 2:222.

3. New York, 1924, p. 97. Subsequent references will appear in the text.

4. Lewis Jacobs, *The Rise of the American Film* (New York, 1939), p. 378. According to Peter Bauland in *The Hooded Eagle* (Syracuse, N.Y., 1968), Kaufman's bizarre comedy sketches for the Marx Brothers in such works as *The Cocoanuts* are full of expressionistic devices (p. 94). The motion picture version of *The Cocoanuts* (1929) was codirected by Robert Florey, who had earlier made such expressionist films as *The Love of Zero* and *The Suicide of a Hollywood Extra.*

5. Denis Johnston, *Collected Plays*, 2 vols. (London, 1960), 1: 18. John Galsworthy, quoted in "In Praise of Satire," *New York Times* editorial, November 12, 1925. *The White Monkey* (New York, 1924), p. 137. When Charles Horace Malcolm's *Bachelor's Brides* appeared on Broadway in 1925, most critics noted the similarity of its anxiety dream to that in *Beggar on Horseback.* For a recent discussion of expressionism in *Beggar* see Paul T. Nolan, *Marc Connelly* (New York, 1969), pp. 48–53.

6. In *Twenty-Five Best Plays in the Modern American Theatre*, early series, ed. John Gassner (New York, 1949), p. 497. Subsequent references will appear in the text.

7. *Our Changing Theatre* (New York, 1931), pp. 105–9.

8. *Harvest of My Years* (Indianapolis, 1943), p. 304.

9. New York, 1928, p. 30. Subsequent references will appear in the text.

10. David S. Lifson, *The Yiddish Theatre in America* (New York, 1965), p. 433. Another Yiddish group that gave expressionistic productions was "Unzer Theater" (1924–25), which staged Ansky's *Day and Night* and Pinski's *The Final Balance.*

9—The Legacy of Expressionism

1. An even closer anticipation of key images in another absurdist play—Samuel Beckett's *Waiting for Godot*—is found in these lines from Lawson's *Marching Song* ([New York, 1937], pp. 52–53):

PETE   What's your name?
LUCKY Lucky.

PETE   You don't look lucky.

LUCKY   [*Laughs*] Don't you see that ole rainbow, honey-bright rainbow fitted snug around my neck? You don't see it, huh? [*He comes close to* PETE. *His voice suddenly loses all its warmth.*] You don't see no rope neither? Look close, Mister, then you see the marks where the rope burned deep. That's why I'm lucky!

PETE   [*Slowly, staring at the rope in his own hands. . . . Holding out the rope.*] Is this strong enough to hang a man?

LUCKY   [*Takes rope and tests it.*] That, snap like a string.

See also the final scene of Arthur Adamov's *Ping-Pong* and William Saroyan's *The Ping-Pong Players* (1942).

2. *The Theatre of the Absurd* (Garden City, N.Y., 1961), p. 259.

3. *The Theater and its Double* (New York, 1958), pp. 30, 99. For a skeptical assessment of Artaud's expressionism see Eric Sellin, *The Dramatic Concepts of Antonin Artaud* (Chicago, 1968), p. 140, n. 147.

4. The interview with George Sklar and Albert Maltz was conducted in Los Angeles, California, in the summer of 1966.

5. Hallie Flanagan, *Arena* (New York, 1940), p. 213.

6. Letter to Hans Maria Wingler, April 3, 1951, quoted in Oskar Kokoschka, *Schriften: 1907–1955*, ed. Hans Maria Wingler (München, 1956), p. 459.

7. *Act One* (New York, 1960), pp. 73, 102.

8. New York, 1957, p. 39.

9. Norfolk, Conn., 1949, p. ix.

10. Louis Calta, "Albee Lectures Critics on Taste," *New York Times*, March 23, 1965, p. 33.

11. Mardi Valgemae, "Albee's Great God Alice," *Modern Drama*, 10 (December 1967), 267–73.

12. Megan Terry, *Viet Rock and Other Plays* (New York, 1967), pp. 155–56, 201–2.

13. Oscar Cargill et al., eds., *O'Neill and His Plays: Four Decades of Criticism* (New York, 1961), p. 5.

14. Joseph Wood Krutch, *The American Drama Since 1918*, rev. ed. (New York, 1957), p. 240. Ezra Pound, "H[ugh] S[elwyn] Mauberly" [*sic*], *Dial*, 69 (September 1920), 284.

Selected Bibliography

This highly selective bibliography of secondary sources does not include the items referred to in the notes or in the text.

Angus, William. "Expressionism in the Theatre," *Quarterly Journal of Speech*, 19 (November 1933), 477–92.

Block, Anita. *The Changing World in Plays and Theatre*. Boston, 1939.

Broussard, Louis. *American Drama*. Norman, Oklahoma, 1962.

Brown, John Russell and Bernard Harris, eds. *American Theatre*. New York, 1967.

Büdel, Oscar. "Contemporary Theater and Aesthetic Distance," *PMLA*, 76 (June 1961), 277–91.

Canby, Henry Seidel. "The Expressionists," in *Definitions: Essays in Contemporary Criticism* (second series). New York, 1924. Pp. 20–30.

Cheney, Sheldon. " 'Expressionism' in German Theatres and Our Own," *New York Times Book Review and Magazine* (April 30, 1922), pp. 5, 26.

Dickinson, Thomas H. *Playwrights of the New American Theater*. New York, 1925.

Downer, Alan S. *Fifty Years of American Drama, 1900–1950*. Chicago, 1951.

Elwood, William R. "An Interview with Elmer Rice on Expressionism," *Educational Theatre Journal*, 20 (March 1968), 1–7.

Flexner, Eleanor. *American Playwrights: 1918–1938*. New York, 1938.

Fulton, A. R. "Expressionism—Twenty Years After," *Sewanee Review*, 52 (Summer 1944), 398–413.

Gagey, Edmond M. *Revolution in American Drama.* New York, 1947.

Gassner, John. "What's Happened to Expressionism?" *Theatre Time,* 2 (1950, no. 2), 37–41.

Gorelik, Mordecai. *New Theatres for Old.* New York, 1940.

Groff, Edward. "Point of View in Modern Drama," *Modern Drama,* 2 (December 1959), 268–82.

Hoffman, Frederick J. *The Twenties,* rev. ed. New York, 1962.

Macgowan, Kenneth. "Expressionism in the Theatre," *Vanity Fair,* 17 (October 1921), 55, 88, 90.

O'Neill, Eugene. "The Playwright Explains," *New York Times* (February 14, 1926), sec. 8, p. 2.

Sievers, W. David. *Freud on Broadway.* New York, 1955.

Simonson, Lee. "Down to the Cellar," *Theatre Arts Magazine,* 6 (April 1922), 119–38.

Turner, Darwin T. "Dreams and Hallucinations in Drama of the Twenties," *CLA Journal,* 3 (March 1960), 166–72.

Turner, Darwin T. "Jazz-Vaudeville Drama in the Twenties," *Educational Theatre Journal,* 11 (May 1959), 110–16.

Waith, Eugene M. "Eugene O'Neill: An Exercise in Unmasking," *Educational Theatre Journal,* 13 (October 1961), 182–91.

Warnock, Robert. "Beggar on Horseback," in *Representative Modern Plays: American.* Chicago, 1952. Pp. 24–31.

Whitman, Robert F. "O'Neill's Search for a 'Language of the Theatre'," *Quarterly Journal of Speech,* 46 (April 1960), 153–70.

Young, Stark. "The Hairy Ape," *New Republic,* 30 (March 22, 1922), 112–13.

Index